BUSINESS JOURNALISM

HOW TO REPORT ON BUSINESS AND ECONOMICS

Keith Hayes

Apress·

President and Publisher: Paul Manning
Acquisitions Editor: Jeff Olson
Developmental Editor: Robert Hutchinson
Editorial Board: Steve Anglin, Mark Beckner, Ewan Buckingham, Gary Cornell, Louise Corrigan, James DeWolf, Jonathan Gennick, Jonathan Hassell, Robert Hutchinson, Michelle Lowman, James Markham, Matthew Moodie, Jeff Olson, Jeffrey Pepper, Douglas Pundick, Ben Renow-Clarke, Dominic Shakeshaft, Gwenan Spearing, Matt Wade, Steve Weiss, Tom Welsh
Coordinating Editor: Rita Fernando
Copy Editor: Deanna Hegle
Compositor: SPi Global
Indexer: SPi Global
Cover Designer: Anna Ishchenko

Distributed to the book trade worldwide by Springer Science+Business Media New York, 233 Spring Street, 6th Floor, New York, NY 10013. Phone 1-800-SPRINGER, fax (201) 348-4505, e-mail orders-ny@springer-sbm.com, or visit www.springeronline.com. Apress Media, LLC is a California LLC and the sole member (owner) is Springer Science + Business Media Finance Inc (SSBM Finance Inc). SSBM Finance Inc is a Delaware corporation.

For information on translations, please e-mail rights@apress.com, or visit www.apress.com.

Apress and friends of ED books may be purchased in bulk for academic, corporate, or promotional use. eBook versions and licenses are also available for most titles. For more information, reference our Special Bulk Sales–eBook Licensing web page at www.apress.com/bulk-sales.

Any source code or other supplementary materials referenced by the author in this text is available to readers at www.apress.com. For detailed information about how to locate your book's source code, go to www.apress.com/source-code/.

Apress Business: The Unbiased Source of Business Information

Apress business books provide essential information and practical advice, each written for practitioners by recognized experts. Busy managers and professionals in all areas of the business world—and at all levels of technical sophistication—look to our books for the actionable ideas and tools they need to solve problems, update and enhance their professional skills, make their work lives easier, and capitalize on opportunity.

Whatever the topic on the business spectrum—entrepreneurship, finance, sales, marketing, management, regulation, information technology, among others—Apress has been praised for providing the objective information and unbiased advice you need to excel in your daily work life. Our authors have no axes to grind; they understand they have one job only—to deliver up-to-date, accurate information simply, concisely, and with deep insight that addresses the real needs of our readers.

It is increasingly hard to find information—whether in the news media, on the Internet, and now all too often in books—that is even-handed and has your best interests at heart. We therefore hope that you enjoy this book, which has been carefully crafted to meet our standards of quality and unbiased coverage.

We are always interested in your feedback or ideas for new titles. Perhaps you'd even like to write a book yourself. Whatever the case, reach out to us at editorial@apress.com and an editor will respond swiftly. Incidentally, at the back of this book, you will find a list of useful related titles. Please visit us at www.apress.com to sign up for newsletters and discounts on future purchases.

The Apress Business Team

This book is dedicated to the hundreds of thousands of journalists worldwide who toil tirelessly and fearlessly, sometimes in very hostile conditions, to bring transparency, honesty, and veracity to the stories they report on, investigate, and write.

Special praise goes to those who have worked alongside me in difficult situations and volatile environments and who have become loyal friends and committed colleagues.

Contents

Preface

This short book was originally meant to be a guide for journalists working in those countries that have recently embraced democratic processes and are transiting to open market economies.

But it is also useful for student journalists, young journalists with little experience in a newsroom, and any journalists who are changing direction from general news reporting to the specialty of business and economic reporting—or from print to television or radio. Journalism students will find it useful as a primer for good journalistic practice and as an aid to their studies.

It is a short book, deliberately so. There are many hefty volumes written by others on this and other media topics, which are suitable for those studying journalism at a higher level. This slender tome is designed for those who are already experiencing the rigors of journalistic practice—late nights, early mornings, and interrupted weekends—as well as those students who need a short and simple book to refer to quickly, especially when assignments are due.

It can also help those who have already learned that ill-tempered editors, critical publics, and embarrassments caused by lapses in concentration are the normal pressures of the profession they have chosen. It is designed to assist those who want a book to which they can make quick reference—a book that can stay with them when they are racing to meet a deadline, or running after a finance minister who is loath to talk.

This book is a combination of notes on good reporting practice, tips on practical reporting skills, and an assessment of the role of the media in a transitional economy. It also contains suggestions on specific knowledge that journalists should have in generally reporting business and the economy. It is not intended to be a complete instruction book on business reporting. Rather it focuses on those issues raised by many burgeoning journalists themselves. Some of these reporters are already business journalists, and others are those who have recognized the importance to civil society of accurate and impartial economic reporting.

The content of the book reflects many specific economic problems identified as being important to journalists in democracies struggling to develop an open market economy, and underscores how intelligent, thoughtful, and sensitive media should make the reporting of such issues a priority.

These prescriptions apply equally to journalists caught up in the chaos caused by the financial crisis in the latter part of the decade that began in 2000, when the major headlines were almost always about business, finance, banking and economies and the mess they were in. This is especially so following the specific global financial events of 2008, which spilled over into another year and a year after that and a year after.... The events in those years are likely to have a profound effect on the majority of global economies for many more years to come and will thus remain newsworthy.

The book is meant to be of help to journalists who are active in all countries and who have the responsibility of telling the civil population what is happening to their economies and how it affects them. Indeed, there is material contained in these pages that journalists just entering the profession—anywhere in the world—might find useful. I hope so.

Journalists are storytellers. But in telling the story, they not only need to tell it well but also make certain they are telling the facts as they find them and indeed as they understand them. The book therefore contains material on good journalistic practice, as well as specific advice on how to report on various elements that make up economic and business news.

Many news media enterprises in maturing democracies seem to forget the value of training. For that matter, it is often given low priority in Western countries. Sometimes editors think they are all-knowing and see the idea of instruction as an affront to their own experience and skills base. But business journalists know, or should know, that proper training schemes, refresher courses, and external performance monitoring are key in making any major corporate business successful. The training budget in large companies and in effective governments is generally substantial. It is surprising, therefore, that media companies in emerging economies are often resistant to training, as are smaller enterprises in the burgeoning Western media sector.

Getting back to basics and avoiding complacency is an important objective for all news media and should be pursued as an active policy. That is why I have included in this book elements on the basic principles of journalism. Those who have been reporters or newspeople for long periods of time are the first to acknowledge the usefulness and effectiveness of going back to basics. These are the journalists who become great reporters and don't get left behind in a morass of mediocrity.

The book has two sections. The first has several short chapters on a number of key issues that business journalists should always have in the forefront of their minds, such as how to write a good news article or how to spot a story. The second section digs deeper into the knowledge and techniques required of a business journalist, such as understanding the basics of macroeconomics or corporate finance, and it is a more detailed guide to good practice and application of the business news discipline.

The book is a guide. It does not purport to be an A–Z of business skills, economic know-how, or operational practices of business journalism. Becoming a top business and economic journalist requires patience in garnering deep knowledge from experts such as brokers, economists, analysts, and bankers. In other words, "doing it," which is the industry mantra for becoming a good journalist, also applies to business journalism.

I hope this book helps in each individual's development and creates the thirst for practicing business journalism, which many—I among them—believe to be the industry's most exciting form of reporting.

I acknowledge the support and assistance of the British Embassies in Yerevan, Minsk, and Bosnia; the Foreign and Commonwealth Office in the UK; Internews in Yerevan and Lithuanian Journalism Centre in Vilnius; Behar Zogiani in Kosovo; Randy Walerius, Atom Margaryan, Graham Addicott, and Barry MacDonald; and Eugene Rembor, Tracy Marsh, and all the support staff who made this book possible. I also acknowledge Jeff Olson, who against the odds thought there was room for a book of this sort and persuaded his colleagues to publish it; my book editor Rita Fernando, who put up with a good deal of curmudgeonly behavior from me; and Jennifer Lynn, who reminded me that the differences in British and American English were no excuse for sloppy writing.

I also acknowledge all the other numerous training manuals and courses that address some of the issues raised in this book.

I am not saying anything new. I subscribe to the epitome of journalism stated in a UPI handbook of yesteryear:

- Tell them.

- Remind them that you have told them.

- Then remind them that you have reminded them.

This volume pays tribute to that adage and indeed is intended not so much as an original work but as a reminder of the basics and skills required of business and economic reporting.

About the Author

Keith Hayes enjoyed a successful career as a journalist and broadcaster, working at leading news organizations CBC, BBC, CNBC, PBS, and Reuters. He was Head of News at CJOR, a Canadian radio station in Vancouver, before joining BBC news in Northern Ireland. He led a business news unit at Reuters, which involved being bureau chief and London anchor for the American daily coast-to-coast business television programs *Morning & Nightly Business Reports*. He ended his broadcast career at CNBC in London.

While at Reuters, he designed and implemented for The Reuters Foundation numerous business news training courses for overseas journalists. He subsequently helped to develop television stations in Russia and Kosovo and ran journalist training courses in Hong Kong, India, Poland, Russia, Ukraine, Armenia, Georgia, Bosnia, Lithuania, Latvia, Kosovo, Serbia, Macedonia, Romania, Nigeria, Ethiopia, Jordan, and London.

He is a partner in First Freedom Distribution, which gathers news video footage for global distribution, and is a part-time senior lecturer and trainer in journalism in London. He has written numerous training manuals for young journalists and reporters working in transitional economies as well as a book on business reporting for television. He is married with a daughter and two grandchildren and is a member of London's Travellers Club. His natural tendency to rebellion comes from living in the English town of Lewes, which was the home for many years of the American revolutionary Tom Paine.

Acknowledgments

The people who helped in the creation of this book are too numerous to mention in full. Hopefully those left out will somehow forgive me and demand a drink in compensation for my oversight when next we meet.

Mention must be made of Melissa Conti, who was my co-anchor on *Morning Business Report*; Randolph Walerius, my business journalism mentor at Dow Jones; Simon Brooksbank for his wonderful insight into the use of pictures; Graham Addicott of First Freedom TV Productions; Jim Boulden of CNN; Ann Turner, now in Timor Leste; Behar Zogiani, a fearless journalist in Kosovo; Danijela Kozina, the bright future of Bosnian journalism; Alexander (Sasha) Sambuk, who keeps me sane in Russia; former Media Commissioner in Kosovo, Anna Di Lellio, who did the same in Pristina; Olga Sushina in Russia, whose father looks after my tomatoes in his greenhouse when I am away from Moscow; and Joel Duku, who does the same in Damaturu, Northern Nigeria.

Many journalists contributed to my professional development: former APTV chief, Stephen Claypole; rambunctious Reuters editor, John Sutton; and Reuters Foundation boss, Jo Weir, who started my training career by sending me to far-flung places.

Mention is made in this book of the clubs where business was done in the early 19th century, and members from two of these clubs helped by making general observations during its writing. Thanks to the Cosmos Club in Washington, DC and also to the London's Travellers Club, which was described by a London Times diarist as "a club for faded diplomats, MI5 spies and thirsty journalists!"

And I thank the many restaurateurs, barmen, and waiters who filled with interesting chatter those lonely moments experienced by most journalists who work in the field.

I am grateful to you all.

A Brief History of Business Journalism

Business information was generally available in the popular coffeehouses of London and New York in the 18th and early 19th centuries simply by people talking to each other. Those conversations gave rise to printed news pamphlets and eventually newspapers. The *Financial Times* was founded in 1888; and *The Wall Street Journal*, still America's biggest selling newspaper, came out a year later. So it was business and trade that helped create the journalistic profession of which you are—or wish to be—part.

As trade began to rapidly increase, the great institutions began to grow. The coffeehouses were no longer good enough or reliable enough for trade purposes, so The Bank of England, the London Stock Exchange, The New York Stock Exchange, and the London Corn Market were established, which made the trading of goods and commodities more formal.

The first true business journalist was German-born Paul Julius Reuter, founder of the famous newswire service Reuters. He was a failed businessman when he arrived in Britain; but by 1851 he had a flourishing news business, supplying prices and information on corn crops from the great wheat-growing countries in central Europe to the commodities markets in London.

Reuter realized that whoever was the first to provide information on the wheat harvests from the corn belts of Europe to the London markets, so prices could be set, would provide a truly useful business news service—and a profitable one. Other companies in the same business of providing information to London about harvests on the great wheat-growing regions of Russia and Ukraine took several days to get such information back to Britain because they used transport over land to convey their reports. The telegraph cables only reached from London to Belgium, so Reuter replaced his regular messengers, who would deliver the news on the harvests from Eastern Europe to the wire heads, with carrier pigeons. These birds flew to the wire service offices in Belgium, where the information on commodities was passed on to London by wire. It now only took a day to get the information from countries such as Ukraine to Britain. Reuter became wealthy.

The first business news operation, which was to grow into a news and financial information Goliath, had started.

The First Business Newspapers

The early newspapers, precursors of the *Financial Times* and *The Wall Street Journal*, began to grow in both New York and London at about the same time as Reuter developed his market news centers, but for different reasons.

Coffeehouses as a venue for sharing news and information gained in popularity during the 17th century and became forums for business information in the 18th and early 19th centuries. The private gentlemen's clubs of London served a similar purpose for the rich and titled. To this day, the dining rooms of London clubs are known as the "coffee" rooms. From that came printed news pamphlets and eventually newspapers. In New York, however, the famous pamphleteer Tom Paine took fledgling newspapers to new heights in urging the colonists to rebel against the English crown. The issue was taxation, so Paine was an early business journalist as well as a rebel.

But now the great institutions were beginning to grow. The Bank of England, the London Stock Exchange, the London Corn Market, and the trading of other goods and commodities became more formal. Trading moved out of the coffeehouses into these institutions and so did the news about prices and buyers. The business press was born.

20th- and 21st-Century Business Press

Although London was a great marketplace, the social revolutions of the late 19th century curbed open market policies and legislation far more in Britain than in the United States. As a consequence, America developed as an open trading nation far more rapidly than London. The average 20th-century American citizen owned stocks and shares, played the market, and made private investments in business.

This revolution didn't really happen in Britain until the early 1980s with the open market policies of Margaret Thatcher, who encouraged ordinary people to own shares, especially in newly privatized enterprises. As a result, business news was far more prominent in the *New York Times* than the *London Times*.

That didn't mean that business news wasn't needed in the UK: far from it. But ordinary general newspapers conveyed that information until the advent of the *Financial Times* (FT) in 1888. Even then, it was the turn of the century before the FT flourished as a business newspaper.

This book makes much of the recent financial crisis of the past decade. However, one of the most famous about-faces of open market policy had tragic results in 1920s America.

For a variety of reasons, recession set into the US economy. The press of the day urged the government to do something about it and hounded the administration into passing the Hawley–Smoot Tariff Act of 1930. This act created legislation that raised American tariffs on overseas goods to such an excessive level that there were few imports. The theory was that the United States was big enough to produce its own natural resources and to contain an internal market big enough to support a manufacturing sector that would produce its own goods and create significant employment.

Such policies rarely work and, in this instance, they were a huge disaster, triggering the Great Depression in the United States and creating such poverty in other countries that the whole industrialized world was affected. Nowhere was this more true than in Germany, where unemployment stoked the rise of National Socialism, which triggered the start of the Second World War. It was a shameful period in history, and the involvement of the business media in badgering politicians to introduce protectionist trade policies put a black mark against journalism for several decades afterward.

In the UK, meanwhile, socialism gained ground. After the Second World War, trade unions took a giant grip of business, including newspapers, radio, and television. The concept of a *closed shop*—which means a worker needed a job to be a member of a union but could not get a job unless a member of a union—led to cronyism, corruption, and the right to manage businesses being taken away from management and effectively handed over to trade union officials. Britain became uncompetitive, with new technology scorned and workers' rights becoming more important than efficient business practice. Vast numbers of people were required to produce newspapers and television programs because trade unions insisted on overtime restrictions and dictated which employees could write and report news and who could use technology such as film and videotape editing machines, so that growth in the media sector was stunted and the news industry began to decay. TV reporting crews in New York, for example, were composed of three people; while in Britain, news gathering took double and sometimes treble that amount of people.

That changed in the late 1970s with the election of Britain's first female Prime Minister, the firebrand Margaret Thatcher. Determined to return Britain to being a strong trading power, she confronted the various trade union organizations, sometimes violently, until most restrictive practices disappeared. She also introduced a massive privatization policy, selling off most state-owned enterprises and making ordinary citizens shareholders.

The advent of this new open-market policy in the UK saw a deregulation of the electronic media. As a consequence, radio and television programs—and indeed channels that were forerunners to such TV stations as CNBC— mushroomed. And because many ordinary folk now had an interest in the fortunes of major businesses by virtue of owning shares in them, interest in business news grew rapidly.

Unfortunately, TV business news is expensive and many programs closed down with the recession of the late 1980s. They flourished again with a resurgent economy, only to see sharp cutbacks, some bankruptcies, and curtailment of activity in the new millennium. Analysts forecast that business news would bounce back as the economy improved, and these forecasts proved accurate; media, especially business media, have flourished in the second decade of the 21st century. However, traditional media are facing a new challenge from new media, online journalism, and the new fashion of getting information off the Web.

Other developments worth noting have added to the importance of business media over the years. Satellite delivery of text and pictures has helped the speed of information. The Web has enabled widespread distribution of business information, and when television properly conquers the challenge of how to properly use the Web as a distribution platform, which is not too far off now, the impact will be even greater.

Despite these developments in delivery technologies, business journalism is not going away. Quite the contrary: business media are very important to the operation of stock markets. When companies are publicly owned—that is, when shares are held outside the company—legislation demands full and open disclosure of information. Business agencies such as Dow Jones and Reuters are extremely important to this disclosure, and both the stock markets and individual companies work closely with them to ensure that information is released at exactly the same time to avoid any charges of concealment. As stock markets spring up over the Balkans, Eastern Europe, Central Europe, Asia, and the Middle East, this relationship is becoming increasingly important to public relations practitioners in industries listed on stock exchanges. Related media activity is seeing a boom.

The business press has become very influential in modern financial markets. It can deliver news at the speed of Superman, without having to pause in a telephone booth for a change of underwear. As top financial agency reporter Randolph Walerius points out in this book, a fraction of a second can be vital to how markets react to the release of company or economic news. Media provide the conduit for distributing that news, analyzing it, and even forming conclusions from it. Business media act as monitors to companies inasmuch as they can focus on weak or ineffective management, growth of competitors, factors that can alter prices or costs such as hurricanes, famine, drought, wars, or other disasters that may disrupt the activities of a free and open market.

If Reuter had had computers rather than pigeons, perhaps the history of the business press might have been a lot different. But he didn't, and despite that he changed the face of business reports and thus changed the nature of business reporting.

One thing is for certain: he found being a business journalist in the 1800s just as heady and exciting as I find it today. My hat is off to Paul Julius Reuter, and a plague on those faceless bureaucrats who still want to get rid of pigeons in Trafalgar Square!

Establishing Good Journalistic Practices

Putting Business Reporting into Context

Why should anyone want to be a business reporter? Is reporting on industry and the economy an important business?

The role of the business journalist has taken on increasing importance over the past few years as conjunction with major economic changes have roiled the world. And it will become even more important as economic crises continue to shake and reshape the social environments of almost all the countries of the free world.

So business and economic journalism is arguably the most exciting branch of journalism today and will remain journalists' most solid career choice going forward.

The Business Journalist

What's required of you, the business journalist?

You must be completely accurate. You must be completely impartial. You must have a nose for news. Business journalism is mostly investigative work.

And investigative journalism has the biggest effect on the everyday life of the ordinary citizen.

As a business reporter, you dig out and report on issues that can immediately or ultimately affect the average person's predicaments and choices. The business journalist is the professional who alerts and informs ordinary people about such personally interesting issues as job losses and opportunities, rising medical costs and declining housing prices, food shortages, and the factors affecting investment income and paychecks.

■ **Note**   Business journalists must be impeccably accurate and impartial. And you must understand your role in society—you are reporting on stories that affect many people in the community one way or another.

Who, What, Where, When, How—and Why

All cub reporters are taught that their stories must answer the standard descriptive questions: Who? What? Where? When? How? They are also taught to ask the overarching sixty-four-thousand-dollar question: Why? Yet too many members of the journalistic profession around the world fail to ask that big question and thereby fail in their first duty as journalists.

Why do so many journalists fail to ask, "Why?" Some journalists are simply lazy. They perform what is scathingly called "protocol journalism"—get the press release and just print it or broadcast it. In so doing, such journalists do no more than an office drudge would do at the copier machine. So why pretend to be a journalist?

Others simply do not understand that as journalists they must report the impact that stories are going to have on their readers, viewers, or listeners—in other words members of the community at large. And yet that is their responsibility; that is their commitment to their fellow human beings.

In business journalism, reporters need to ask, "Why?" They need to dig out the facts. They need to report accurately on everything they can, because business and economic journalism reveals important things that affect everybody. And they need to analyze it intelligently and contextualize it usefully.

A Cautionary Tale

On a visit to eastern Ukraine, I was entertained at the offices of a major newspaper by senior staff members. During the conversation, they told me about a substantial overseas investment in a steel plant there.

The size of this investment was big enough to warrant international attention, so I contacted a colleague at Dow Jones Newswires, the international business and financial news agency in London. His editor put a reporter on the story and swiftly the news went around the world.

Essentially, the story was that a Swiss steel company had decided to invest $100 million in two casting machines in the steel plant. These machines would eventually produce 2 million metric tons of steel plate a year.

International investors were keen to know such information because it gave them signals about the wisdom of investing in a region about which they knew little. Why did the Swiss invest in this machinery? Is the total output of this plant going to increase? Is the steel market expanding? Are there new export factors that triggered this move?

Those questions needed to be asked because if any of the answers were in the affirmative, then the overall steel production of the region would expand. Lacking training, the journalists in the news office I visited hadn't thought to ask them. It was a prime example of protocol journalism.

Yet the implications of this news were vitally important to the local population. It might have been the harbinger of more employment, the rejuvenation of plants, an injection of cash into the community, and the return of prosperity. On the other hand, the local consequences might be negative: Would the machines do the work once done by manual labor, such that jobs would decrease and local people would be thrown out of work? Would local shops get more business or less? Would food producers see an increase or decrease in their revenues? What effect might the investment have on tax revenues?

These questions would have been running through the minds of thousands of people who in one way or another would be affected by this event in the steel industry, and it is up to the business reporter to provide the information. What on the surface seemed a dull economic story might in fact have provided dozens of human interest stories and yielded critical information to people with hopes and fears about the investment's impact on their daily lives. When communism collapsed, the welfare state went with it. So just what would this event mean to the local populace if workers were made redundant? How would their families support themselves?

This incident was sadly symptomatic of much journalism in mature as well as emerging democracies: write what you are told and ask no questions. But the role of journalism in any country is to inform, to ask questions, to provide answers, and to sharpen social awareness or even crusade on social issues.

The Importance of Business and Economic News

The biggest recent growth in media has been in .business and economic news, especially since the financial crisis in 2008 and the ensuing problems experienced by almost every country around the world. Although business and economic reporting has always been an important component of media output, the demand for business news has grown as free market principles have taken hold around the globe, and so have the number of journalists who report it and the editors who see it as an important part of their news coverage. Business news is the cutting edge of investigative journalism and increasingly makes the major headlines in newspapers and the lead stories on TV or radio. Reporters and writers of business news are accordingly ever more important.

Business news is also essential to the operation of stock markets. When companies are publicly owned—that is, when shares are held outside the company—legislation demands full and open disclosure of information. Business news agencies such as Dow Jones and Reuters are an integral part of this disclosure. Western stock markets as well as individual companies work closely with them to ensure that information is released at exactly the same time to all media to avoid any charges of concealment.

Stock markets are springing up all over developing regions such as the Balkan/CIS, so it is important that reporters in such countries establish a relationship of trust and cooperation with market management. Most of these stock exchanges don't have the sophistication of Western market establishments, but journalists can assist in their development by introducing reporting skills and practices when writing stories about their local exchanges.

The Need for High Journalistic Standards

Business reporters have a big responsibility to ensure that they observe the general rules governing the practice of journalism. Being a competent, honest, and impartial journalist is essential when reporting on business, the economy, and government. If journalists get their facts wrong or let opinion take over from independent reporting, they may cause people to lose their jobs, prevent inward investment, or encourage corruption and incompetence in government or corporate affairs.

Reporting on business, the economy, and financial matters doesn't mean that a journalist has to be a businessperson, economist, or accountant. In fact, most people in these professions make bad reporters. What journalists do is tell a story. In the case of specialist reporting such as business, journalists need to have a fair knowledge of the background to their story, but they do not need to be experts. Reporters must never be afraid to ask. And they need to be good storytellers, first and foremost.

▓ **Tip** Top Journalists are news gatherers and disseminators, assessing what information is important and then relaying it to the public in as appealing and revealing a fashion as possible. Therefore, writing skills, broadcasting talents, voice development, and even modes of dress are important.

Code of Practice

Media talks constantly about the need for freedom of the press, but that freedom can be secured only by responsible reporting. Freedom demands responsibility.

Journalists are not usually closely regulated by law. Unlike medicine and the legal profession, it is possible to practice journalism without being required to follow a compulsory professional code—hence the international concern when the British media were threatened with government regulation following the Leveson inquiry into phone hacking.

Here are a few guidelines that the responsible and sensible journalist should always remember. These guidelines are substantively included in voluntary codes in a number of countries with a free press.

- Journalists should never give or take a bribe or gift in any form.

- Journalists should not let politicians, businesspeople, public relations officers, or spin doctors play confidence tricks on them.

- Journalists should not allow themselves to be coerced. If the story isn't an honest one, it's no good to anyone.

- Journalists should never allow someone who claims they know the owner of their newspaper or broadcast station to put pressure on them.

- Journalists must be impartial and should not be financially, politically, or emotionally involved in the story they are reporting.

- Journalists should be fair and honest, and they should not mislead interviewees, sources of information, or their audiences.

- Accuracy is vital. Published information must be correct. Conflicting information should be assessed and placed in context. Mistakes should be publicly corrected.

- Reporters should provide subjects a fair opportunity to reply.

- Financial journalists must refrain from taking personal advantage of privileged knowledge.

- Reporters should ask themselves how a journalist should react to public relations departments, including government spokespeople and politicians. How satisfactorily and impartially do these departments handle the flow of information to the media?

- Modern news gathering techniques mean journalists must react to the speed of current technology and reporting modalities. Nonetheless there is never any excuse for not producing accurate, presentable, and timely news. Accuracy, credibility, and truthfulness must never be compromised by the need to be "first with the news."

- Confident in her journalistic due diligence, a journalist must vouch for her story and robustly defend it against criticism or claims of inaccuracy.

Business journalists face trying pressures in both new and old economies: bribes, promises of holidays, new cars, and many other blandishments to write a story that is not quite in keeping with the facts. Resist giving in to such temptations. Maybe you won't be found out, but the feeling of pride in a story well researched, well written, and above all accurate and true is much greater than looking at a brand new automobile and knowing you sold your professional integrity to get it.

An essential tool by which you make sure you have tried your hardest to establish the facts is conducting interviews with the key players associated with your story.

How to Conduct Interviews

Most journalists will have to interview people to gain the information they need. Here are some points of good practice to follow:

- Remember to prepare for the interview; do your homework on a story and the issues involved.

- Ask questions directly, properly, and as simply as possible. Don't try to impress an interviewee with your knowledge of the subject: news people are there to gain information, not to show off.

- Set the interviewee at ease, listen to the answers, and respond to the conversation. Don't interview by rigidly following a list of questions you have noted down before the interview. The only question you really need to prepare is the first one.

- Stay in command of the interview. A reporter has no divine right to receive answers—but he or she has a perfect right to ask the questions. Discourage interviewees from saying, "No comment." Point out that it makes them look as if they have something to hide.

Tip TV reporters should become skilful in editing the text of an interview on location. You may not have time to do anything but a quick phone call or you may not have electronic editing facilities available when you return to base.

After you've conducted your interviews, it's time to write the story.

How to Write the Story

First, identify your audience. Who are you writing for? Who are you broadcasting to? Is your news agenda geared to the public who want to know what is going on? Make sure you are not writing because, as a professional, you think you know what they need to hear or read. Don't be drawn into speculation or giving a "personal" view. All stories must be based on facts.

Rule The golden rule of journalism is that there is no golden rule. Journalism is not an exact science; each story needs a different treatment and a different angle. Much of journalism is about debating the issues and looking at them with a fresh pair of eyes.

The watchword for writing a news story is "keep it simple—or KISS (Keep It Simple, Stupid.) Use words that the public will understand, not those that will impress the boss.

Discuss story angles with colleagues. For example, what is the impact of a workers' strike? Will it trigger unemployment? What does that mean to the local economy?

▓ **Tip**   When writing a story, bear in mind the limit on the number of words that you can use. It will be different for each medium—text, television, and radio—but there is always a restriction, so make sure every word counts.

Keep these guidelines in mind when you apply the familiar formula that a story must have a beginning, a middle, and an end. To hook the viewer or reader, think of how you might begin telling a story to someone standing near you— "A big steelworks in London has gone bust!" or "Stocks took a hell of a dive today!" The language might need improvement, but these lead sentences do grab the attention of the reader.

After you have established a lead, select the key facts to back up your story. Use sentences that are short enough to be understood easily but not so simple that critics could say you've come straight from kindergarten. Do not make them so complex that they are incomprehensible unless read several times. Where possible use the active voice: "The government today announced ..." not "An announcement was made today...."

The onus for clarity is on you, the writer, and no one else. Always ask yourself: do I understand what I'm writing? If I don't, then others will have no chance.

Journalists must also realize that people do not remember everything they are told, even through the very powerful medium of television. In assessing and writing stories, remember to tell them, remind them that you've told them, and then remind them that you've reminded them.

Finally, be ruthless in editing your own piece. Do not try to cram in every fact you have researched, and avoid clichés and jargon. See how the story reads once you have finished it, put it aside for a little while, then re-read and if necessary tweak it to ensure it is telling a story accurately and intriguingly.

▓ **Note**   If you publish something that is factually wrong, put a correction on the record. Journalists are human. They make mistakes. Admit to an error, correct it, but don't be overly defensive about it.

Last Thoughts

This chapter is a general guide for business journalists illustrating the way they should go about their work.

The following chapters in this book are designed to help you understand some of the key financial and economic issues of which you need to be aware. It's hard work. And remember—the really professional way to report on economic and business issues is to ask the experts.

Key Points

- You don't have to be an economist to be a good business reporter.
- Never be afraid to ask for information.
- Be a good storyteller.
- Follow the good practice code.
- Prepare for interviews.
- Identify your audience.
- KISS.

Writing Effective Business News

The business journalist must be exceptionally careful in practicing basic reporting skills because the slightest error can have a profound effect on readers' lives.

On one occasion a journalist at a major newswire agency reported that UK interest rates had been raised. The markets were thrown into a panic because there had been no indication from any reliable source that this was about to happen. In fact, the news was about *Irish* interest rates and the reporter had made a simple error. The mistake was corrected after about 60 seconds; but in that time, millions if not billions of pounds had shifted on global markets, stock prices went haywire, and directors had been ordered to assemble for urgent meetings in head office boardrooms. This simple journalist error had monumental consequences.

■ **Caution**   One of the major dangers in the practice of business journalism is that familiarity breeds contempt. Many journalists cut corners, bend under the pressure of deadlines, and produce sloppy work through overconfidence. Don't be one of them!

In addition to being hypervigilant about accuracy, business journalists must take extreme care in other areas related to writing. In this chapter, I describe not only the basic skills a business journalist must have, but I also include tips for writing effective news leads (also known as *ledes*) and stories.

■ **Note**   Throughout this book, the lead sentence or paragraph of a story will be spelled *lead*. As an old hack, I still use *lead*, as indeed most other old hacks do. The obsolete Middle English spelling *lede* was revived to distinguish the *lead* referring to a lead-in sentence from the differently pronounced *lead* referring to the thin strip of metal used in the days of hand-typesetting to separate lines of type. *Lede* crept into the US news business in the 1970s and is still confined mostly to the United States. So readers must forgive the clash of culture (as well as spelling) here. The main lesson to be learned from this is that a good news story has conflict, and this is as good a journalistic conflict as they get!

The Basic Skills of the Business Journalist

The practice of good basic journalism is of huge importance to the business journalist. In undertaking the role of a business reporter, it is wise to live by the code of basic skills employed in every major newsroom in the world. These skills, though not always directly related to the writing process, will make you a better journalist and ensure that your stories have maximum impact.

Keep Good Records

First and foremost, it is essential that you keep a full and accurate record of the information you gather in day-to-day newsgathering activities.

In the old days, the notebook was king. Today it is more likely to be the iPhone or digital voice recorder, electronically recording each word, both question and comment.

■ **Note**   Again, here is an interesting clash of cultures. The training for certification by the UK's National Council for the Training of Journalists (NCTJ) includes shorthand as a required course, and this certificate is recognized by the British government and most major UK news enterprises. Yet of all the countries I have worked in, Commonwealth nations such as the UK, Australia, and New Zealand seem to be the only countries that require shorthand of entry-level journalists. Because digital voice recorders are generally not yet allowed in various institutions such as British courtrooms, it makes sense.

The importance of keeping records is obvious. Challenges are made every day about what was said in an interview or as a comment, and journalists above all are open to the charge of misreporting or taking things out of context.

Always ensure that you have a fallback record of what was said in case you later need to establish the accuracy of your reporting. Never slough off establishing who you are interviewing and where the interview took place.

REMEMBER THE BASICS

I was once in a news meeting with a now very famous broadcast journalist who sat frozen with fear as the deadline for the arrival of a very tough news editor drew near. He muttered to his colleagues that he was likely to have his head ripped off because he had just come back from an interview and had forgotten to ask the name of the interviewee.

Keeping your head on your shoulders is essential, both for the veracity of your work and the safety of bodily parts from angry news editors.

Know Your Style Guide

Almost all major and most smaller newsrooms have style guides. This is the way the newsroom reports material in its writing or broadcasting of news. Style guides are intended to be a map, guiding the journalist in the "way we do things around here." For example, style guides prescribe house usages such as when to capitalize a job title and when to spell out numbers instead of writing numerals.

In Britain, each publication, radio, and TV newsroom has its own style guide, drawn up by editors both past and present. In the United States, editors and publishers tend to favor a more national approach, often using *The Associated Press Stylebook and Briefing on Media Law*.

Double-Check Your Work

Use the library. Mostly digitalized now, reference materials are readily available through the computer terminal. But to gain information from yesterday's newspapers, which can be an important news source, especially in smaller outfits, the newspaper is usually stored on a shelf or hung up on a peg, giving easy access to the publication. Use this facility as a double-check against error. Many a report has had copy in Monday's newspaper that a stock lost 5 percent of its worth, only to find reference to that in Tuesday's paper as 50 percent.

The Internet is a wonderful research aide, but again be careful and double-check. Output information is only as good as input information, and if the person who fed the data into the machine makes a mistake, then it can be multiplied in a thousand places and a thousand times by those who simply "cut and paste"—not to mention the mischievous who delight in misleading journalists through website rubbish.

I once asked a class of young journalists to research the history of the story of Dick Whittington. Historically, Whittington was a 13th-century Lord Mayor of London. Folklore had it that he came to London as a vagrant accompanied by his cat and ended up in high office. The students used the Internet for their research. Their stories contained "facts" that Whittington was a real person (true) and had one to four wives, several cats, and left a fortune or died penniless. All this, they claimed was on the Internet. But what was really true?

Ask Questions

Before writing a word, understand what is required of you and, if in doubt, ask before going about a story. Too many journalists don't understand what the story is that they are being asked to cover. As a consequence, they often report on a totally different set of facts than their editors planned. If you don't understand your brief, ask the editor until you are sure you know what the story is about.

Never be afraid to ask, especially if you are dealing in stories from Wall Street or the City.

■ **Note** There are two common terms in business parlance which I suppose could be considered jargon. But they are so commonly used in financial circles that there's no sense in fighting them. *The City*—the City of London district in central London also known as "The Square Mile"—is often used as a metonym for the UK's financial services sector, which is largely based there. Likewise, *Wall Street* is a street name that is used as a metonym for New York's financial district and more broadly for the US financial markets as a whole.

When I converted from general news to business journalism, I knew nothing about the financial sector. But I was no spring chicken and asking questions was second nature. I recall asking a City of London guru about bonds and what a *coupon* was. There was an embarrassed silence in the newsroom, but the guru patiently explained to me how bonds are priced, sold, and yield interest—and indeed that *bond* is another name for *debt*.

That guru became a good friend and has often remarked that I was refreshing as a journalist because I asked the basic questions without embarrassment, while others often pretended to know what they were talking about and misconstrued a story as a result.

Don't be afraid to ask, and call me stupid if you want to.

Keep Your Opinions to Yourself

Don't give way to personal opinion. Making sure your story is factually correct is your responsibility, and you must give a full and balanced view of what you have seen and learned. Some UK reporters, for example, came under considerable criticism when the 2008 recession began for using terms such as "the government's savage spending cuts" or "hitting the poor who can't afford to feed themselves." Possibly these statements were true, but without supporting evidence, they became editorial comments.

Get the facts. And in doing so, once again don't be afraid to ask people with specialist knowledge—such as analysts, brokers, asset managers, and bankers—what it is you want to know. They are often as pleased that you have asked them for simple advice as you are to get the precise technical information.

▓ **Rule** If you use an exact quote, you must attribute that quote to the expert who said it.

Writing Effective Leads

Every story begins with a lead. The lead is the introduction to your story and often contains its most important point or points. The job of the lead, once written, is to entice readers or viewers into your story.

The style for a lead that is used today came from the days when the main means of communication was the telegraph, or wire, that stretched from coast to coast across the United States—and, hence, the term *newswire services* and such newspaper titles as *The Daily Telegraph*.

Newspaper and television news organizations observe different rules when writing a lead. For newspapers or wire text, sometimes a descriptive paragraph can lead into the story. This example of a lead is from a British middle-market tabloid newspaper.[1]

> *Feeling blue may not be all bad when it comes to enjoying a good night's sleep. Those with bedrooms this colour tend to get the best rest and wake feeling happy and positive.*

The writer was clever with words, but it is a newspaper lead that backs into the story. A broadcaster would never get away with backing into the story but might rather say: "Researchers say that the color of your bedroom walls can dictate how well you sleep."

For broadcast news writing, the most important information is always in the "top line" of the story. A writing pyramid can then be constructed, with ever more information being added in descending order of importance.

The format for radio and television is constructed as a pyramid for a variety of reasons, but the most important is that the audience needs to be "captured"—compelled to listen to the story. The traditional bold headline to a newspaper story isn't available to the broadcast journalist (although of course headlines are used in a different way), so the news reader has to barge into the story straight away.

Newspapers can indulge in an inverted pyramid in which a more relaxed and less direct introduction can be used. Not all newspaper editors accept this format, however. The former crusading editor of the *Sunday Times*, Sir Harold Evans, claimed that newspapers should follow the pyramid style of the broadcast media. And some do.

---

[1] Jaymi McCann, "Want a Good Night's Sleep?" Daily Mail, May 15, 2013. http://www.dailymail.co.uk/news/article-2325476/Want-good-nights-sleep-Find-colours-use-bedroom-avoid-decent-kip.html. For other examples of good leads, see Ray Massey, "Petrol Sharks Pile On Agony for Drivers," Daily Mail, May 16, 2013. http://www.dailymail.co.uk/news/article-2325804/Petrol-sharks-pile-agony-drivers-After-price-fixing-raid-BP-Shell-damning-report-reveals-traders-driving-costs-motorists.html; and Danielle Douglas, "Regulators Put Together Tougher Restrictions on Bank Payday Loans," Washington Post, November 21, 2013. http://www.washingtonpost.com/business/economy/regulators-put-tougher-restrictions-on-bank-payday-loans/2013/11/21/44c86316-52d3-11e3-a7f0-b790929232e1_story.html

THE ORIGIN OF THE LEAD LINE

Early newswire copy was written in the pyramid style because journalists using the wires over vast distances such as those from say Los Angeles to New York were well aware that the vagaries of storms, animals, and vandals could disrupt the wires at any time. So they got out the most important part of the story first. They created what is now described as a "lead line." Thus the "wire" stories could still be understood even if the writer was unable to deliver more than just the first sentence and the wires went dead thereafter.

Here's an example of a pyramid-style lead line:

President Reagan has been shot.

The story has been told, even if more detail is eventually required.

So a style was created that was both necessary because of hostile environments, but crowd-pleasing because the news was spat out early in the story. Facts, figures, and more detail were then added on in order of importance to provide a longer and explanatory story. Both reader and copy editor could stop reading whenever they liked but could still get the basic information the reporter had related.

So the basic style of a short, sharp first paragraph in news copy was set many years ago and still has its advocates today.

EVERYTHING BUT THE KITCHEN SINK

Young journalists often fall into the trap of trying to put every fact and figure they have researched into the first line or sentence. I always called this sort of lead as having "everything in it but the kitchen sink." As an editor, when I saw this sort of headline, I would yell across the newsroom "Kitchen sink!" Reporters immediately knew what was wrong with the story and rewrote it quickly.

Leads in Authoritarian Regimes

There is a great temptation in journalism in the new democracies to follow the old style of communist journalism. In authoritarian regimes, the ruling class was always far more important than the actual news story. So a newspaper article would begin something like this:

> *President Georgy stood outside the presidential place today in a dark blue suit, a red tie, and with his wife at his side. The marble arches of the palace glinted in the morning sun, reflecting the aura of the presidential party as a crowd of onlookers pressed up closely. The presidential palace, which was designed by the president's grandfather, is located on Palace Street, noted for its avenue of trees, leading up to the gilt-coated entrance doors. The President announced he will resign.*

Almost any reader, anywhere in the world, would have given up on the story before it had even begun. Sadly, there is still a tendency in some of these countries not to change, which is worrying because the circulation of readership of all newspapers can be as low as one percent of the population and few ask why this is so.

Finding Your Lead

Finding a lead line can sometimes be a problem for even the most experienced journalist. To overcome this difficulty, try thinking of how you would start to tell the story to a friend or your family if they were with you and asked what stories you were reporting that day:

> *The U.S. Federal Reserve has boosted interest rates.*

or

> *Champion steel works has gone bust.*

These might not be ideal lead lines in themselves, but with a bit of tampering, they can be molded into a lead line that grabs the audience.

Make it short, sweet, and to the point.

Things to Keep in Mind When Writing Your Story

Once the lead is written, each additional paragraph will add more detail to the story. Once again simplicity is the key. Use straightforward language that is easy to read. In addition, keep the following rules of good writing in mind:

- *Wherever possible, use the active voice.* "The cat chased the mouse" is more dynamic than "The mouse was chased by the cat."

- *Avoid using jargon and other technical language, especially when writing about complicated subjects.* For example, IMF is *International Monetary Fund* and WTO is *World Trade Organization*—so say so, at least when the terms are first used. You know what the acronyms stand for, but your reader might not know or at the very least has to think about it, thus interrupting reading flow.

- *Spell it out.* Some newspapers and magazines include in their style guide a descriptive word or phrase for companies to make sure that there is no mistake. For example, use the phrases "automobile manufacturer Ford Motors" or "insurance company Aviva." This is not a bad habit to get into, no matter what your own style guide might suggest.

- *Consider avoiding emotive words, especially if they are flagged by your style guide.* For instance, Reuters tries to avoid the word terrorist, preferring *guerrilla* instead on the grounds that one man's *terrorist* is another's *freedom fighter*. Don't carry your quest for neutral words to silly extremes, but do think about the emotive side of journalism and whether you are intimating some bias by an ill-chosen use of vocabulary.

THE IMPORTANCE OF ACCURACY IN BUSINESS NEWS

Writing news is a skill to be learned. Writing business news is one step further because the choice of words, the use of numbers, and the importance of accuracy means the business journalist must be extra careful. Sloppiness can have an effect on people's lives, and unintentional mistakes can't be covered by an apology if a slip of the tongue or an error of fact puts people out of work or costs them their life savings.

Practice, Practice, and More Practice

Writing good news copy for text, TV, or radio might seem like a minefield to those of you just starting out. I suppose it is. But take heart that it will eventually become second nature—like riding a bicycle.

Like any skill, writing news copy needs first of all to be understood and then practiced regularly. Be prepared to take constructive criticism from editors or mentors. For example, one of my nephews decided to study journalism at a university (not always the best place to get to grips with media reality). But his mentor was, like me, a grizzled old veteran of a UK national newspaper not noted for being gentle with cub reporters. My nephew told me that he was extremely proud of his first piece and then devastated when it came back with red lines through almost every sentence. But he stuck with it and is now a successful young reporter at a leading UK regional newspaper. Persistence is invaluable in the news game.

Too many entry-level journalists think that they will become famous columnists five minutes after walking into a newsroom, only to find the reality is quite different. Ambition is a wonderful thing and I would never try to dampen enthusiasm. But to get to the top requires hard work, and novices need to plow through lots of routine tasks before being assigned to the seemingly dullest, most boring stories. In beavering away at these tasks, they are picking up the skills that must become second nature to them and will hold them in good stead as their careers progress.

Good journalists are made, not born. So while you are stumbling through the maze of journalistic skills—being accurate, developing a writing style, remembering to keep records, double-checking everything, struggling with a lead, and laboring on pyramids—recollect that all the great journalists went through the same ordeal before emerging as masters of their profession.

Yes, the industry is changing. But those who grasp the basics of the profession (some say trade) will find the eventual rewards can be magnificent. My personal journalist hero was Walter Cronkite who, among countless honors, received from President Carter the Presidential Medal of Freedom. Not bad for a man who started out at *The Daily Texan* just like you, worrying about accuracy and style and all those irksome journalistic tasks—mastery of which helped make him a preeminent public figure honored by his country with its highest civilian award.

Key Points

- Keep a record, written or electronic, of all conversations and interviews.

- Know and follow the appropriate style guide.

- Research carefully and don't be afraid to ask.

- Understand how to lead into a story and write the lead line carefully and precisely.

- Avoid jargon and embrace plain language and simple syntax.

Reporting for Different Business News Media

The basics of news writing outlined in Chapter 2 apply to all media, especially business media. The principles of accurate and credible news writing don't vary from paper to paper or from TV station to TV station. What does matter is to know and understand who you are writing for: the nature and construction of the medium concerned.

If you work full-time for a publication, then it is relatively easy to follow an editor's instructions, reflect the signature style of the paper, and cater to its target audience, because everyone else in the company will be doing the same thing. But if you are a freelance journalist, it is vitally important that you acquire a precise and intimate knowledge of the news outlet you are writing for or pitching to.

The Importance of Learning How the Various New Media Operate

The Internet has wrought major changes in the job opportunities for journalists. A plethora of newsworthy and contextual information is available from Internet sources. (Caveat: Never use uncorroborated or unchecked material from anywhere—least of all the Web!) The adoption and dissemination of digital technologies have shrunk the permanent staffs in most print and broadcast organizations. But in tandem with that shrinking trend, the dependence of news organizations on freelancers has increased. Business journalism is one news sector that has generally escaped this shrinkage thanks to the increasing importance of business news across the globe.

All journalists—whether in-house or freelance—should understand the key components of whatever publication or broadcaster they are working for. Nothing is more needlessly painful than having an article or news story thrust back in your face because you failed to understand the nature of the organization employing you.

There are literally tens of thousands of news outlets around the globe, many publishing in a single language and many others in multiple language editions. These outlets can be split into different categories, such as newspapers, magazines, wire services, TV, radio, and online.

This chapter surveys a sample of major news organizations—mostly but not exclusively publishing in English—selected to represent the largest and arguably the most globally influential information services.

Each of these has its own way of operating. Dow Jones, for example, is almost exclusively business and economic news, although it owns *The Wall Street Journal*, which also covers world and general news.

Reuters leans heavily toward business and financial news, but also has a strong TV unit and a world news division. Bloomberg, on the other hand, is best known for its TV news but also has other outlets in print and online. A large part of Reuters' and Bloomberg's businesses involve selling financial information to banks, brokerages, and industry.

The news industry is extremely complex. Journalists need to understand the structure of the news industry and the spectrum of news enterprises in broad terms, as well as the particular profile and market of whatever entity you are writing or working for within a news enterprise.

News Enterprises

The types of major business news enterprises vary a great deal, but they all fall into one of the main media categories described in the following sections: newspapers, newswire agencies, picture agencies (discussed in Chapter 12), TV stations, radio stations, business magazines, and general news outlets that feature business reporting within a general news concept.

Key Daily Newspapers

Three international daily newspapers—*The Wall Street Journal*, *The Financial Times*, and the *International Business Times*—are the biggest business and financial newspapers in the Western world. High-circulation business newspapers in other regions of the world include *Nihon Keizai Shimbun* in Japan and The Economic Times in India. Nationally important business newspapers include Germany's *Handelsblatt*, Australia's *Financial Review*, and Croatia's *Poslovni dnevnik*.

Note Newspaper circulation numbers are a vexed field for comparison. The traditional rule of thumb in the newspaper industry for calculating eyeballs-readership was to multiply the number of paper copies sold by three. The rationale behind this calculation was that each copy would on average be passed among three readers. This calculation technique remains true of printed newspapers but many publications now include on-line readership in their circulation figures, although most show separately the numbers for printed copies and on-line.

These newspapers are all major entities in the business news market, and any journalist intending to report for them needs to be well versed in international business events and news and fluent in the language of publication. These do not constitute a definitive or exhaustive list of business newspapers, but they are representative of the major daily publications that specialize in business news. In addition, almost all newspapers carry some business news— even red top tabloids such as the UK's Sun, better known for its topless Page 3 girls. Some newspapers give much more prominence to personal finance than to business and economic news but, even so, some form of business news is contained in almost all daily papers.

Key News Agencies

In addition to the daily newspapers, important general news agencies that pay significant attention to business and financial news include the following:

- Agence France Press (France)
- Reuters (USA and UK)
- Dow Jones Newswires (USA and UK)
- AP and its TV arm APTV (USA and UK)
- UPI (USA)
- Jiji Press (Japan)
- RIA Novosti (Moscow)
- Xinhua (China)

Most of these agencies have news bureaus in all the major cities of the world to help gather their international news. Dow Jones, for instance, has 85 bureaus manned by more than 2,000 staff members. Of them all, Dow Jones is the agency that concentrates almost solely on business news, followed by Reuters.

Business News on TV

TV has seen an upsurge in business news outlets. The two most significant are Bloomberg TV and CNBC, which are totally dedicated business news channels.

Other TV companies such as Canada's Business News Network, the UK's Sky News Business, the US's FOX Business News, and India's ET Now (tied to the Economic Times) are also serious players.

Business Magazines

Notable US business magazines include *Barron's*, *Bloomberg Businessweek*, *Forbes*, *Fortune*, and *Harvard Business Review*. Mainstream UK business magazines include The Economist, The Business Magazine, Euromoney, Marketing Week, and Investors Chronicle. A host of trade magazines publishing at various intervals target particular business sectors and professional specialties—accounting, railways, hedge funds, maritime insurance, book publishing, and so on.

▨ **Caution**   Almost all business magazines need freelance submissions, but beware—the editors know what they are talking about and look for articles from reporters who also have intimate knowledge of the subject. Be sure you know what you are talking about before writing for them.

Business Radio

There are a large number of all-news radio stations that assign substantial airtime to broadcasting business news, especially in the United States. BBC-affiliated radio stations in the UK give extensive coverage to business matters, as does the London-based private radio station LBC. But for the most extensive coverage anywhere in the world, Bloomberg's name again crops up with Bloomberg Radio. Many of these business-oriented radio stations are online, whereas regional radio (sometimes called local radio) limits news to that which is of interest to local listeners.

Other Publications and Broadcast Media

Many publications, television stations, and magazines that are geared toward general news nonetheless devote time or space to business and economic news, including Al Jazeera, Russia Today, France 24, CTTV, CNN, CBS, BBC, CBC.

SO YOU WANT TO WORK AS A FREELANCER?

Because there is such a wide spectrum of news media outlets, the best advice for a reporter is to either work for one of them to learn their style, read one or two avidly to report as a freelancer, or become a specialist in some part of the business and finance sector so that your stories are filled with technical knowledge that makes your tale unique. Chapter 2 outlined the styles of writing used for various types of media. That advice holds true for any story writing you might do, so apply those guidelines to any reporting for the various media detailed in this chapter.

Broadcast Journalism

Many people believe print journalism and television news are related. It would be foolhardy to argue they are not, but they are distant cousins rather than blood relatives. The very nature of television—and radio for that matter—makes the requirements of news gathering, news priorities, and story selection different from print. The techniques of writing, composition, production, and presentation for television and print bear few similarities, and there are few common tools required to do the two jobs.

▓ **Tip**   The differences between print and broadcast journalism do not mean newspaper reporters do not make good broadcast journalists or vice versa. But those who venture into television from print should be prepared for a whole new way of doing things.

The Development of Broadcast News

Radio and television developed differently in the United States from the way they did in Britain. Early in the century, major US news agencies refused to allow newfangled radio to have access to their copy. So broadcasters were forced to develop a whole new method of gathering and disseminating news. That gave rise to the beast known as the *broadcast journalist.* Cross-fertilization between American newspaper, radio, and television was not unknown, but it was—and still is—the exception rather than the rule.

In the United Kingdom newspaper people were key players in the early development of broadcast news. This traditional link has remained. As the broadcast industry has become global and more complicated, however, broadcast journalism has become an accepted profession in its own right.

Best Practices for Broadcast Journalism

There are broadcast-specific best practices to be adopted and assimilated by those who aspire to broadcast journalism—whether they are print journalists wanting to move to broadcast or professionals from other parts of the television industry.

The broad differences that "scribes" should note in writing for different business news media is that newspapers generally require more in-depth reporting than broadcast pieces. In text stories, all questions should be answered in telling the tale (Chapter 2). Newspapers generally have the space to do this, whereas television news (documentaries aside) has very tight time constraints.

Generally, business news for text afford the option of writing some descriptive text before hitting the real story, whereas broadcast news do not afford that luxury. Still, newspaper reporters shouldn't get carried away and neglect putting the most important information close to the top.

▓ **Note**   A key element of television news is the mini-production known as a *package*—an item usually reported by a journalist on location and one of the most frequently used broadcast news methods.

In modern newspapers and magazines, business news need more visuals than in the past to explain complicated stories. Reporters need to develop the skills and habits for creating and commissioning photos, graphics, and tables.

REPORTING FOR RADIO

Radio of course needs writing that is for the listener's ear, rather than the reader's eye; sentences must be crisp and short. In radio, news stories can generally only last for two minutes, and that includes a sound bite (an excerpt from an interview). The script will contain less information than a print story, so the picture building is very important. So sound effects, especially in business stories, are usually required. Sounds of buses, planes, factories, people talking, conference noises, the New York Stock Exchange bell, and telephones ringing—all add to building a visual image in the listeners mind.

"Writing to pictures" is an essential technique for TV journalism (Chapter 9). But abstract business issues often do not lend themselves readily to TV visuals. Reporting on a specific business is easy enough. A camera crew can shoot "custom" pictures of the enterprise by being on site with the reporter. But a story about inflation, which is more of a high-level concept than a visible event, calls for clever picture selection.

The same old visual clichés—money rolling off a printing press, the New York Stock Exchange opening or closing, the Bank of England frontage, a dealer in front of a computer screen, or shoppers going through checkout —weary viewers through repetition. Worse, jaded producers call up stock footage that is anachronistic or anomalous, such as rolling a Christmas shopping scene in a July story.

Think out the words carefully. Don't echo the pictures in words. A clip of coal miners leaving the pit should not have a script that says, "Coal miners left the pit this morning…" As with radio, time is of the essence: stories generally run from about a minute to three minutes, and that includes a sound bite of at least 20 seconds.

Try to keep the story interesting with wide-angle shots, cutaway shots, and panning. But beware when you pan. If you don't leave two or three seconds before each pan, editing will be a nightmare and result in jump cuts, a phenomenon known to make viewers dizzy.

Finally, add credibility to the story by doing a *piece to camera* (PTC) in which you speak directly to the viewers through the camera. This instills trust in the story by proving to viewers that you, the reporter, were actually on the scene.

Reporting for Online Journals

More and more reporting is done for online journals. These generally should be anything up to 500 words per page. This can be in a free-flowing style, but all other journalistic rules apply. Get them wrong and you may trigger consequences no less disastrous to yourself, your employer, the subject, business, and your readers than if you got them wrong in print journalism. No matter what the medium, business reporting is a serious business.

Key Points

- Before you begin reporting, you need to understand the nature of the publication you are writing or broadcasting for.

- There is a wide range of newspapers, magazines, TV, and radio that cover business issues.

- It's important to understand the differences in producing business news for print, TV, and radio.

- Always use medium-appropriate techniques that add credibility to your story.

Establishing Sources of Information

So how does a business journalist go about getting the information he or she needs to write a competent and well-balanced story?

Well, a business journalist is like any other journalist really. He or she has to get information by asking, digging for, and analyzing information. Is this tough? Yes, but surely that is the very essence of journalism, the very reason most reporters choose this profession, the root of the challenge of being a journalist. Getting information is not simple, and I would not suggest to budding business reporters that it is.

This chapter will show you just how challenging—and rewarding—your job as a business journalist can be.

Rights and Responsibilities of the Media

As members of the media, businesses journalists must keep the following points in mind:

- Business journalists have no divine right to receive answers, but they have a perfect right to ask questions.

- Business journalists are not infallible, but they must try to get to the truth of a story when perhaps there are many who would prefer to obscure that truth.

- Business journalists have a responsibility to report a story—and if they can't get cooperation from business, then they must find other ways to get the information.

Fortunately, businesses journalists have many opportunities to gather information, starting with their contacts.

Contacts: The Life Blood of the Journalist

As a journalist, you need to build as good a picture of what is going on as possible. In pursuing a story, you must avoid being drawn into speculation or giving a personal view. That doesn't mean that the reporting stops if the owner of a business refuses to talk or answer your questions. There are many ways for you to discover what is going on in an industry. Speak to competitors, union representatives, workers, bankers, or any number of people from your contact list.

■ **Note**   As your career progresses, it is essential that you build up your contact list. These people may one day become key sources of information.

To ensure success in your stories and in your career, it's important to build up a regular list of contacts comprised of government officials, other journalists, entrepreneurs, business club members, bank personnel, business owners, politicians, and representatives of such organizations as NGOs, trade associations, international bodies, unions, and chambers of commerce. Invest the time in getting to know what's going on even when it's not worth reporting; get an overall picture, be well informed, and also be respected by your contacts.

Every journalist should keep a list of helpful people and their contact details—telephone numbers, e-mail, addresses, and so on. You should also try to find out people's private home and mobile telephone numbers, so you can call them out of hours or out of the office, where it may be difficult for the person to speak freely.

Obviously, some of your contacts will be more important than others. Politicians, top business figures, key union personnel, police chiefs, mayors, and charity leaders all need to be on the contacts list and all spoken to on a regular basis. Others will not figure prominently in day-to-day stories but nonetheless should be cultivated for background, leads, and network.

Contacts are a reporter's life blood. Journalists need to nurture contacts, stay in regular touch with them, and make them almost friends. Only by developing a network, gaining their trust, and doing a first class job on the story when using their information will you be able to access material other reporters don't have—and be able to break news stories.

As reporters we depend on tip-offs; we need information from people who live, work, and play in walks of work and life that journalists have little knowledge of and even less access to. Sure, reporters must follow up and check the accuracy of these leads. But without the lead in the first place, there is nothing to follow up.

Tip   Don't accept any information as fact except from a proven reliable source, unless you corroborate it from at least two other independent sources.

THE IMPORTANCE OF CONTACTS

In my early days as a young reporter in Vancouver, I was handed the police beat—a seat at the "cop shop," as it was known. It was a great place to learn the tricks of the trade, and I made the most of it. I got to know not only police officers but also lawyers from the adjacent courts.

I was busy on the phone one morning, all alone chasing stories on a slow news day, when a young lawyer I had got to know stuck his head into the pressroom and with a cheeky grin said, "Courtroom Three in five minutes."

I duly presented myself on the press benches in the courtroom and looked at the docket to see that the case involved a murder. On the surface it seemed a fairly routine case and was indeed a preliminary or "first" hearing.

The bare outlines of the case were read out, and then my lawyer friend said that the prosecutor was going to ask for the death penalty. There was a collective gasp around the courtroom, even from the judge. The death penalty in Canada had been abolished five years before. There was no death penalty: or so I and most others on that day thought.

In fact, the Canadian government had placed a moratorium on hanging for five years, not an outright ban. This particular court case was five years and one day after the start of the moratorium, which the bright young lawyer had discovered was now lapsed because the cabinet in Ottawa had forgotten to renew it.

It was a great story and an exclusive one to me. It of course had all sorts of repercussions for government, for the legal system, and for that matter was a wake-up call to hardened criminals who now faced death by hanging if the murderers in this case were found guilty.

In the event, the Prime Minister called a cabinet meeting very quickly and extended the moratorium.

But it was a great story, and it came to me by nurturing contacts.

Human Nature

Human nature also plays a large part in providing news tips. People like to see their names in print or have their faces appear regularly on the television screen. One business analyst told me that his firm valued publicity so much that it was written into its employees' contracts that they must attempt to appear on business programs a set number of times each year or forfeit their bonuses.

Contacts are often key figures holding important positions in well-known organizations, but they may also be secretaries or even taxi drivers. It is striking how many people who might be considered insignificant nevertheless see and hear what is going on and can provide nubs of information that can turn into really good stories.

The wise reporter will try to ensure that such willing interviewees have really got something newsworthy to say or are not exaggerating a circumstance to become "famous" for five minutes.

Most good journalists develop a "nose" for such informants and can very quickly intuit the difference between the publicity seeker, the time waster, and the contact who adds real value to a story and believes that the public has a right to know what is really happening.

Tip Don't get so caught up in looking at the specific story that you close your eyes to the "social factor" that you can inject into stories. Never underplay the importance of the community and the contribution your story can make to life in that community.

Emergency Services

Most American and Canadian radio and television stations have a very thorough system of checking on news stories.

Each day calls are made at least twice to hospitals to follow up on stories. For instance, when a story is initially filed as a motor vehicle accident, the names of the people involved and the hospital to which they are taken goes onto a list. Those names are checked every day to see whether the condition of the patient gets worse or better. If a patient dies, then the story changes and becomes reportable.

Emergency services are always the targets for daily phone calls. In the US, it is very likely that reporters will have a pressroom in a major police station. In the UK, many reporters will check a police contact at least once a day. In most newsrooms there is a list of calls to be made by the desk duty journalist, which will include some if not all of the following:

- police department
- customs
- highway/traffic police
- traffic control
- fire department
- rescue service
- ambulance service
- hospitals
- coastguard
- mountain rescue
- cave rescue
- weather centers

Some newsrooms listen in to the radio transmissions of the emergency services, which is acceptable in America but notionally illegal in the UK. Sometimes in the US, police dispatchers alert the press to an incident by saying quite plainly—"Commercial media please note"—and giving relevant details of a stolen car or a bank robber.

EMERGENCY SERVICES DISPATCH: THE D. B. COOPER HIJACKING

I was on duty in a Vancouver radio station on the night of the famous D. B. Cooper hijacking and given a blow-by-blow description by the King County Sheriff's office as the plot unfolded.

D. B. Cooper was the name given to an unidentified man who hijacked a Boeing 727 aircraft in the airspace between Portland, Oregon, and Seattle, Washington, on November 24, 1971. He demanded and was given a $200,000 ransom, then parachuted out of the aircraft somewhere over the Washington State countryside. He was never found or properly identified; and, apart from a few notes, the money was never recovered. The case remains the only unsolved air piracy incident in American aviation history.

That story would never have been reported in real time as it happened had it not been for good contacts and regular checks by desk journalists.

You may well ask why a business journalist should bother with emergency services. The fact is that the immediate story might not be of that much interest. But newspapers and broadcast bulletins are full of cutbacks in police funding, fire stations being shut down for budgetary reasons, or ambulance services becoming inefficient because of lack of staff. These are all good business stories and often come to light because the business reporter has developed the same contacts as his or her general news counterpart.

■ **Note** Never underestimate the knowledge and skill that you as a reporter will acquire as a specialist correspondent. Over a period of time, reporters will find they have extraordinary access to industrial, business, political, and community leaders, which will give them knowledge far beyond the boundaries of others.

Forward Diary Systems

A *forward diary system*, in which important stories are logged for action at a certain date in the future, is often used. Sometimes the date is a specific time when an event is going to happen, and sometimes it is an anniversary. In either case, it's a good source of potentially breaking news.

There are commercial diarists such as the London-based Future Events News Service (FENS), which has a substantial staff doing nothing else but searching for upcoming events. FENS offers dates of important events in its World, Business, Entertainment, and National sections, covering the UK, North America, Asia, and Middle East. The diarists sell the lists contained in the diary to news organizations to assist with planning for future news events, and it is widely used by global media. This helps alleviate the need for onerous phone work. FENS is a major international news events organization; but many cities—for example, Washington, DC—list domestic events taking place, and these are also useful aids to future planning.

▧ **Tip**   Useful as commercial diaries are, good journalists keep tabs on events from their own contacts and only supplement a look ahead with information from services such as FENS.

Once it is announced that the president or queen or other head of state is to be present at a place or event, then it is logged in the newsroom for an alert to be made so an editor can assign reporters, resources, and other require-ments to ensure proper coverage is given according to the importance of the story and the pertinent protocol for handling the press corps.

The White House provides the press corps a press room, reporting facili-ties, and a close relationship with the President's press office. Number 10 Downing Street, in contrast, has no such press facility. There is a press office with information officers working for the prime minister and the government, but journalists are invited in for a news story and are not given access as an absolute right.

Since threats and a mortar bomb attack on Number 10 in the late 1980s by the Irish Republican Army, Downing Street has been blocked to the public, and the press needs a special pass just to be allowed to stand outside the front door. My colleagues and I have spent many miserable hours in the pouring rain outside the famous black door waiting for the prime minister of the day to appear to make a statement or introduce a visiting head of state.

The press corps in the Houses of Parliament is treated quite differently. There is a press room, a press bar, a press gallery inside the debating chamber, and for a special group of journalists called "lobby correspondents" access to members of Parliament (MPs) in the Members Lobby, a circular domed area set between the House of Commons (lower house) and the House of Lords (upper house), where parliamentarians gather to talk and informally debate. These lobby correspondents have unique access to the MPs and can use infor-mation they are given privately as long as they don't attribute the quote.

For example, a story might open with the lead: "A source close to government said today that a new trade agreement between Britain and the United States could be signed by the middle of next week." The source might well have been the minister of trade himself who wants to alert the country to an imminent trade deal but who won't make an official announcement until the day the deal is to be signed.

But the real point is that no UK organization, public or private, is under any obligation to provide facilities or lines of communication to the press, TV, or radio if they don't want to. Most do so because it is in their interests to have good relations with media. But there is no obligation.

The News "Patch" or "Beat"

General reporters in searching for news should carve out a "news patch" also known as "beat." The "patch" for a business reporter is more environmental than geographic. The business news patch might include contacts at stock brokerages, banks, institutions such as the Bank of England or The Federal Reserve, and insiders at large corporations and businesses.

Then there is the opportunity to have special patches within a patch. My own were the air and beverage industries. I had great contacts within British Airways, plane makers Short Brothers (now Bombardier), and ship builders Harland and Wolff, who diversified into building "air bridges"—the walkways between terminal buildings and aircraft when you board or leave airplanes.

I likewise had contacts with brewers, distillers, soft drinks manufacturers, and the famous stout maker Guinness. It didn't mean that I was exempt from reporting on and indeed knowing about other things. My job as anchor for PBS's Morning and Nightly Business Reports demanded that I be familiar with the whole of the business and finance sector. But my specialties were drinks and airplanes.

I have flown in new aircraft on maiden British Airways flights, including the Concord, toured Boeing's works in Seattle, and watched the Flying Boxcars coming off the assembly line at Short Brothers in Belfast. I interviewed a Russian pilot who was displaying a spy plane at the famous Farnborough Air Show. He instructed me not to touch a red lever in that particular cockpit because it was the trigger to send the seat shooting out of the plane into the air in the case of something going wrong. I sat very still during that interview.

On another occasion I was sent to a small wine shop in London's Covent Garden to interview a man who was auctioning off a red wine that was fetching several hundreds of dollars a bottle. The story behind the price was that a wine called Le Pin had been given a top American wine critics' maximum rating in 1982, but with the proviso that it should be drunk immediately because it was not good for "laying down" for future use. The wine was expensive (but not outrageous) because only 700 to 800 cases were produced annually by a small French vineyard.

In 1996, someone discovered some cases that had been mistakenly kept back, and the same wine critic declared he was wrong and Le Pin 1982 was better in 1996 than when it had been bottled. The wine world went mad and the few cases left, numbering dozens rather than hundreds, created a bidding war, sending the cost skyward. I can remember calculating that one glass of Le Pin was valued at about $800.

I interviewed the owner of the wine shop handling the sale and generously asked if we could have a glass of wine in our hands while doing the interview. I hastened to reassure him that I didn't expect him to open a bottle of Le Pin as that would mean a very expensive interview for him. But he insisted and I sat sipping on an $800 dollar glass of wine while talking and I was in seventh heaven.

After the interview was complete, the owner's partner came into the store and joined us. The owner immediately said, "Charles, I'd forgotten just how good this wine is. Let's have a bottle for lunch." More than $10,000 worth of wine disappeared in minutes just for the sake of a business news item, and $800 of that was sitting in my stomach!

I hasten to point out that this was not only a wine story, but a commodities story as well. The bidding war on the product bore less relation to the high quality of the wine than to the small quantity of cases left in the world to be bought.

On another occasion, I travelled to Northern Ireland to do a story of a take-over by the massive French drinks company Pernod Ricard of the famous Old Bushmills Distillery. Again, for reality's sake, I ended my piece raising a glass of Irish whiskey to the camera and expressing approval in my face. As a tribute to my usual ability to do just one take in my pieces to camera, I proudly bear the professional sobriquet, "One-Take" Hayes. Yet on this occasion it quite uncharacteristically took me 18 tries to finish off the story!

This digression illustrates how cultivating a "patch within a patch" can result in some in-depth stories that bring no less delight to the reporter than to the viewers.

Your "news patch" can have any sort of focus. It may be a geographical area in which you get to know the community and its concerns. This is especially important for business journalists in severe economic downturns. Why are shops closing? What government support for small business is there, if any? Are there too many types of one particular shop? Is the competition hurting them all, or is there an unusually high demand for whatever they are selling? There are a thousand questions—and perhaps a thousand stories.

Everyday Conversations and Eavesdropping

Don't just limit your contacts to influential people. Sometimes they are a group concealing stories rather than being outgoing with information. Join in conversations in a pub, or coffee bar, shop, or market, or anywhere that people congregate. You might hear a dozen conversations that are inane babble. But you might also get a feel for what is troubling people, such as a bad pedestrian crossing where there are fears that one day somebody might be killed. There is the start of the story, a story that might well lead to reportage on a city's budget and its fiscal priorities.

Reporters should be full of curiosity and should be constantly asking questions. Try to get to the point where people start contacting you with story ideas.

Eavesdropping is another good way of finding out what is going on! It makes you feel like a sneak sometimes, and indeed investigative reporters often lose friends and family because they use information picked up at a social occasion.

THE HEROISM OF INVESTIGATIVE REPORTING

Investigative reporting is a true journalistic art. But before deciding that is a role for you, beware of the cost that many very good investigative journalists have to pay.

Often they work in danger; many times they work on a story for months only to see their hard work fizzle out when the story can't be proved. But mostly the worst cost is to domestic life and how such endeavors can impact on the home and family.

There is, and I suppose always will be, a romance about investigative reporting; and indeed, when the big stories break, investigative reporters become famous and heroes.

Across the Balkans, in seminars of say 50 journalists, 48 participants would declare their intention of becoming an investigative reporter. Our answer to this huge desire to take on the world was for me to produce a friend who was a very good and very successful investigative journalist.

Together we took a little dramatic license over his appearance. But he would enter the room, unshaven, wearing a dirty and stained raincoat, a half bottle of whiskey bulging from his pocket as he shuffled to the podium. It was a bit exaggerated but he would then relate his life as an undercover reporter with no holds barred. Then I would ask the 50 journalists who still wanted to be an investigative journalist. Rarely did more than two hands rise into the air.

Yet one of the best investigative journalists I ever met worked in the Balkans. She was a lady in her early thirties who uncovered massive financial corruption in the government that went to the very heart of the country's finance ministry. She was shot and badly wounded, banned from press conferences, vicious rumors were circulated about her personal life, her young family was threatened, and she had to move home. She was a brave contributor to her country's welfare, yet never received the accolades from fellow journalists, government, or international organizations that she so richly deserved.

Getting to the Facts

So the answer to the question of how does a journalist, general or business reporter, get the facts, is that it is through hard work, patience, and application.

Using the phone, e-mail, and Internet, sometimes for hours on end, is the very basic way to get information. It is simply hard work. Knowing lots of contacts in a whole variety of fields is another. No journalist should be without a little black book, both to keep a contact list up to date and also have a name and number at hand if there is an urgent need to get expert comment.

I keep coming back to the same theme though. Getting news is hard work and needs great application by reporters young and old. Nowhere is this truer than for the business journalist.

The skill for any successful reporter, however, is knowing where to look. And sometimes reporters can't see the forest for the trees. Sources are sometimes so obvious that they are missed or ignored. Everyone who works for a news organization, from the receptionist to the chief executive, should be feeding the newspaper with ideas for stories. So the entire staff is the first resource of newsgathering. Journalists who sit back and wait for news to come to them will rarely succeed. That's why those who have drive and determination make the best reporters. It all sounds so simple, doesn't it? Well, the skill of being a journalist isn't that complicated.

However, understanding the sector can be complex; and while sticking to the basic principles of journalism, young or new reporters need to build their knowledge about business, the economy, and financial institutions as they go along until they have a thorough understanding of the topic. That doesn't mean to say that I have contradicted myself from earlier advice, which is to ask the experts. But the more knowledgeable reporters become in their field, the better they can get information that will enhance and help illustrate their stories.

I have deliberately given examples of important stories that came from good contacts, hard work, and the perils of investigation. These illustrate how to look for news.

But the fact is, for the average reporter, the news comes from simple hard work on the phone, listening to people, and then following up with talking to knowledgeable contacts.

Pretty dull stuff until the story is put to bed. Ah, but then there is no feeling on earth quite like it.

Key Points

- Always remember your responsibilities as a journalist.
- Contacts are vitally important. Make sure you build a useful list.
- Understand human nature as a source of news.
- Consider information from the emergency services for use as a business story.
- Use a forward diary to search for future events.
- Carve out a news patch.

Enterprise Stories

The big business newswire organizations such as Dow Jones and Thomson Reuters put great stock in *enterprise reporting*—reporting that is not prompted by news or a press release but rather is developed from scratch by a reporter digging into sources. Enterprise reporting is especially exciting for any journalist because it is totally his or her own story. The information is not based on the rewrite of a press release or information given out at a news conference. Instead it is about taking a small nugget of information, digging into it, and claiming ownership of it.

Enterprise reporting goes beyond just covering events: it is about identifying something that just doesn't seem to fit and exploring why. Sometimes the clue is a gut feeling of uneasiness or incongruity in response to something read or said; other times it is a simple observation that begs the Why question.

Turning a Simple Question into an Enterprise Story

I was in the city of Calabar in Nigeria with some local journalists. As we were driving along one night, I noticed that on one side of the street, lights were blazing and the area was clean and smart, while on the other side it was dark and shabby.

I casually asked why there was such a contrast in such a short distance as the width of a street. My companions told me, with a nod and a wink, that the one side of the street voted for the state governor, while the other side didn't.

It had not occurred to these journalists (who were not that experienced) that here was a story in the making. Research and a little digging to confirm their thesis could result in a good corruption story and even a story on the state budget. In fairness, once I had fired the starting gun, they were fast out of the gate in chasing the issue down.

That was an enterprise story.

Examples Business journalism is rife with stories exposing faulty and dangerous products, which resulted in manufacturer recalls and reforms of government business regulation. A deluge of stories on price fixing by retailers filed by UK reporters was started off by their spouses' complaints about price hikes in supermarkets.

Turning a Simple Drink into an Enterprise Story

I once was a huge fan of English bitter beer. Offer me anything else and I would reject it with a sneering curl of the lip.

But the warm, dark, hoppy brew is not available in most countries of the world. Overseas, in fact, English beer is treated with the same contempt that Englishmen reserve for lager. (Traveling so much, I have had to drink various shades of lager in many countries of the world that I have, to my eternal shame, lost the taste for English bitter.)

Drinking lager in my local pub, I noticed a steady increase in the cost of lager beer on a fairly regular basis, while the cost of English beer, though rising, did so at a slower pace. I was disgruntled that my beer was disproportionate in cost to the English brew, so I set about researching why.

It proved to be a complicated story, but essentially a whole series of mergers and acquisitions had taken place in Europe, with large international brewers mounting hostile and accepted bids for some of the smaller drink makers.

These acquisitions were widely reported in the business media with a series of interesting stories surfacing over the boardroom battles for control. It was gripping stuff. But it was so gripping that business journalists had failed to note the steady increase in retail lager prices in the inns and taverns of Europe and especially in Britain as a result of these mergers.

A solitary reporter drinking (quite moderately) in a small town bar, however, picked up on this. I had my enterprise story.

■ **Note** Covering breaking news is straightforward, but developing follow-up stories is far more challenging yet peculiarly necessary to the functions of the business reporter, who on a day-to-day basis is dealing with economic, government, and commercial affairs that impact on society as a whole but often conceal uncomfortable truths that need uncovering.

Turning a Simple Question into an Enterprise Story

An indispensable tool for unearthing enterprise stories is the reporter's trained ability to observe. All journalists should observe everything going on around them as a matter of course. To generate good story ideas, they should develop and push their observational skills to the next step by treating their observations not as passive impressions but as continual provocations of the question "Why?"

For example, just filling up at a service station and discovering that the fuel costs a lot more than it did last time you filled up can lead you to questions that cannot be satisfactorily answered without deep investigation. Asking why led to big oil companies being investigated by the European Commission for price collusion in Britain. Plenty of good enterprise reporting helped expose the scandal and pressure the government and oil companies.[1]

■ **Tip** Watch out for change. If something changes, it should trigger the most important "W" question in journalism—"Why?"

From Police Blotter to Enterprise Story

Once the initial alarm bells have gone off, the next step is good old-fashioned digging. Often this means a lot of spadework and a lot of tedious delving for bits of information and data. (But if that tedium turns into an interesting or even spectacular story, there is no greater sense of satisfaction.)

---

[1]See, for example, Ray Massey, "Petrol Sharks Pile On Agony for Drivers," *Daily Mail*, May 16, 2013. http://www.dailymail.co.uk/news/article-2325804/Petrol-sharks-pile-agony-drivers-After-price-fixing-raid-BP-Shell-damning-report-reveals-traders-driving-costs-motorists.html

Enterprise reporting is allied very closely to investigative reporting. The main difference is that investigative reporters start their stories from a bad smell in the air, whereas an enterprise story really does come from a niggling suspicion, a small nugget of information that sets a reporter to uncovering hidden information.

The information that led to the resignation of President Richard Nixon was an enterprise story prompted by a police blotter item that segued into an investigative story.

The initial item was simply a break-in. During the small hours of a summer's day in 1972, a security guard in the Watergate Hotel in Washington noticed a door had been jammed open. He called police and five men were arrested in rooms rented by the Democratic National Committee.

It was simply a story for the police blotter until enterprise reporters discovered one of the burglars was a former CIA man who had notebooks linking him to the White House. That triggered closer media scrutiny and eventually uncovered a "dirty political tricks" scandal that led directly to President Nixon.

Two young reporters from the Washington Post, Bob Woodward and Carl Bernstein, began an in-depth investigation of the incident and are credited with revealing a great deal of unique information as the story unfolded. Later the two reporters revealed that they had an informant inside the White House who was feeding them information. At the time he was nameless and given the epithet "Deep Throat." Much later, Deep Throat was identified as Deputy FBI Director, W. Mark Felt, who was a longtime contact of Bernstein's.

For any journalist, this story is worth examining just because it is one of the great stories in American, perhaps even global, journalism. But it particularly serves to demonstrate how a story can develop from a humble germ to spectacular dimensions. It was also a story that only became possible through good and enduring contacts.

From Mock Press Conference to Enterprise Story

I was training some journalists in Bosnia who asked if we could get a top businessman to come and address us and be the guinea pig for a mock press conference.

Through our contacts at the British Embassy, we persuaded the CEO of a large industrial complex based in Sarajevo to appear. This man was so used to a compliant media that performing such a task gave him no apprehensions. The state-owned company was a newsworthy model because it was being showcased in the government's privatization program.

The executive gave a colorful account of the company, explained that already Siemens, a big German enterprise, was interested in buying it, that it had several contracts in the pipeline, and that all was well with its sale.

The young Bosnian journalists, although very bright and energetic, were also brainwashed by protocol journalism practices and were overawed that such an important man should have agreed to attend their seminar. As a consequence, their questions were almost fawning and certainly not incisive, and if this had been real it would not have contributed to any story about the success or failure of the government's privatization program.

But this executive hadn't counted on having a Dow Jones journalist and a Reuters reporter (me) being there as trainers. The trainee journalists looked embarrassed at first that we should question this important man in such a direct and forthright manner. We were not rude, but we asked about the company's import/export record; who at Siemens the company had talked to; if any prospective buyers or investors had been to visit the plant; how much of the enterprise the government was willing to sell; and several other queries about the sale of the company to the private sector.

To our questions, the CEO either provided very vague answers or proved unable to answer at all. It became painfully obvious that no real effort was being made to transfer the business to the private sector. This led to a second and more interesting story, inasmuch as the government had promised the international community, as part of its economic reforms, that it would follow a robust policy of privatization.

Giving the young journalists their due, the scales fell from their eyes and they followed up on the issue with enthusiasm. A few direct questions—and an enterprise story was at hand.

From Census Data to Enterprise Story

With a bit of hard work, a national census can lead to all sorts of enterprise stories. It means digging, but as a journalist you should be used to that.

Does the data show that there has been a surge in the number of children of primary school age, yet the government budget shows cuts in school funding? If the number of elderly has increased unexpectedly, has the government made financial provision for the increased costs of pensions and nursing care?

These are the sorts of economic stories that can come from the instincts of enterprise reporters. These are good stories that need exposing, stories that only you have, and stories that might provide you with a great scoop.

Use a slow news day to trawl for enterprise stories. You might come up with a yarn that is an important and exclusive story that might just shock your editor into the equally shocking act of praising you.

Key Points

- Look for simple things that seem out of place. This is a good start for an enterprise story.

- Watch for casual tidbits in day-to-day news stories that might turn up an enterprise story.

- Never mock a "mock" training exercise. Real stories can be found there.

- Look for stories hidden in public data such as censuses.

Ethics and Change

I have already made reference to ethics. But it can't be stressed enough that whatever else journalists may do, they must keep any information they get as confidential until they can confirm it is fact.

The reporter must strive to produce the highest possible level in the quality of reporting. Every story has an impact on society—sometimes small, sometimes large. But if the tale is rooted in baseless data or hearsay instead of facts, the impact can cause untold damage, which the journalist ultimately may never be able to put right.

A Brief Definition of Ethics

Commentators define *business ethics* as written and unwritten codes of moral standards that are critical to the activities and aspirations of business organizations. Ethics is about having the wisdom to determine the difference between right actions and wrong decisions. It's an organization's codes of corporate governance, morality standards, and behavior of individual employees and the business as a whole.

Journalists have their own written codes, detailed in this chapter and touched on in Chapter 2, but the basic principle of any ethical consideration of journalism is that a clear distinction must be drawn and honored between news and opinions.

The Importance of a Code of Ethics

As noted in Chapter 1, many countries, professional associations, and news organizations have journalism codes and canons of ethics, conduct, and practice. US and UK codes are very similar, having at their core the principle of good practice as it applies to journalism. Media freedom is an essential clause of these codes which is of particular importance for business journalists; and the right of the public to be informed is essential to good practice.

Big business and financial institutions are not above applying pressure on journalists to turn a blind eye to some practices that are not in the public good. For instance, there have been cases of advertisers threatening to cancel their accounts with a publication if a story that is unfavorable to them isn't dropped.

Such situations are especially difficult for business journalists because they are not really in control of dealing with such threats: it is usually noneditorial management. No one can tell a journalist what to do under these circumstances, but support for colleagues on an ethical level can sometimes ensure that a conflict is resolved in a positive way.

Business reporters need to be especially careful about the way they handle pressures to exempt from scrutiny businesspeople who may be engaging in unprincipled behavior that might cost jobs, damage communities or the environment, and sometimes threaten life itself.

There is no easy answer, but subscribing to a code and an organization such as the Society of Professional Journalists (US) or the National Union of Journalists (UK), which will give some muscle to resisting such threats, can certainly help.

Note   Don't accept gifts or bribes to write a story that is not true, and don't use bribes or false promises to get information. That doesn't mean that a contact shouldn't be allowed to buy a lunch for a chat or that a reporter shouldn't accept a free plane ride to see how an airline works. But don't be put into a position where the information can't be used in a story if it is uncomplimentary to the subject of the item.

Journalists should be free of obligation to any interest other than the public's right to know.

Unbiased Reporting

Impartiality is another important element of ethical values. Biased reporting can easily put a company out of business; this principle is exceptionally important in business news because it is something that a reporter can do without meaning to, through inherent bias or hostility to activities.

For example, an environmental journalist might well feel that carving a new road through a beauty spot is destructive. But it is incumbent on journalists to give a balanced view of the issues and also of the company that is building the road. It is equally important to make sure that any inaccuracies in a story are corrected once identified.

Business, economic, and financial journalists can trigger enormous consequences through their reporting and must always be aware of how influential they can be. Even so-called opinion columnists need to take an ethical stance. Columns that express an opinion must back up the opinion with facts and examples.

BIAS IN EMERGING ECONOMIES

Bias was one of the ethical issues that dogged journalism in emerging democracies as they became democratic. Shackled for decades by authoritarian governments, many media personnel couldn't differentiate between freedom to report on an issue and the responsibility not to write whatever they wanted regardless of journalistic standards.

Adherence to Ethics in Obtaining a Story

One area in which even the most moral journalists have some problems is how to balance the ethical rule that material be obtained by honest, straightforward, and open means with the obligation to investigate a story in the public interest when pertinent information can be acquired only in an underhanded way.

There have been many court cases where journalists have had to argue that they investigated stories in an unethical way because it was in the wider public interest. Courts are sympathetic to this argument; but because it is frequently left to the law to decide the morality of the issue, it is not a course that newspeople should embark on lightly.

Protection of a Source

Another ethical issue that often comes before the courts is concealing the identity of a source of information. Courts are often not very sympathetic to this argument, but reporters can often risk the safety of an informant or the flow of information if they reveal their source. There are many examples of "whistleblowers" (workers who report wrongdoing at work or in government) being fired or demoted after revealing bad practice by industry, government, and other civil society entities.

Within both US and UK codes, right of reply is prominent. This is very pertinent to business journalists because, once again, if subjects of an investigation aren't asked for their side of the story and have a very valid argument for their actions, the consequences can be serious.

ADDITIONAL TIPS FOR ETHICAL STORIES

Here are some additional tips to follow to make sure your work is as ethical as it can be:

Make certain that headlines, news teasers, promotional material, photos, video, audio, graphics, sound bites, and quotations do not misrepresent people or situations. They should not oversimplify or highlight incidents out of context.

Never distort the content of news photos or video. Image enhancement for technical clarity is always permissible. Label montages and photo illustrations.

Recognize a special obligation to ensure that the public's business is conducted in the open and that government records are open to inspection.

Journalists need to be accountable to their readers, listeners, viewers, and each other.

Accounting for Political Beliefs

It is not unusual to find that business and industry take steps to support a political party, through either donations or some other active support. It is not unjust for such donations to be made because the business believes that one party or another, if elected, will deliver an economic- or business-friendly environment suitable for it to trade and prosper.

No journalist should worry about a company's political leaning unless he or she believes that the owner, or the business, or indeed that particular business sector, has been compromised by it. However, if it appears that the business is receiving direct favors as a result of its support—for example, government contracts or state subsidies—then that in itself is a story worthy of the reporter's interest and should be pursued.

■ **Note**   A reporter's own political beliefs should not color his or her reporting, especially if they are opposite views to those held by the businessperson.

It is not unusual that business and even government will be outraged by a particular piece of reportage. That does not mean that the report was incorrect. However, it has not been unknown for businesses to insinuate that reporters they find obnoxious are wrong or have a track record of getting facts confused—in other words, to discredit the reporters and their reports. So it is essential that records and notes are kept, especially on a contentious story, so that the reporter can back up the story and the assertions made in it.

Avoiding Protocol Journalism

Whatever you do as a business reporter, don't indulge in protocol journalism.

Yes, it is essential that you look at every press release that you can. Information comes from them as a source. But don't just repeat a press release. The content of a press release is what a company or government wants to say. It might be factual, or it might be tendentiously slanted toward what the company or government wants people to believe and therefore economical with the truth. Once you have the press release, do research as thoroughly as possible until you clearly understand what the story is, and then use all your journalistic skills to explain to readers or viewers, in the simplest possible terms, what exactly has happened or will happen and why.

Insider Trading

A cautionary note for journalists reporting on stock market news, even for the tabloid press: beware of getting caught up in an insider trading scandal.

Insider trading occurs when an individual or group of individuals who have knowledge about a company that is not generally available to the public trade that company's listed stock. This practice can give such individuals an unfair advantage over other investors inasmuch as they know in advance of the market that a share is about to jump or fall in price.

■ **Note**   In most countries, insider trading is illegal, and the penalties for those who get caught can be very severe.

The definition of insider trading varies widely according to the country. American and British reporters should be aware that many major business news enterprises ask employees to declare what stock they hold in their portfolios. The reporter is not allowed to report on companies in which he or she holds stock. Smaller organizations might not be that fastidious in monitoring their employees' financial affairs, but lack of oversight does not absolve journalists from the same responsibility. Using knowledge about a stock through privileged information gained while researching it is illegal, and the penalties are severe. The cost of losing your job can be far greater than the gain insider trading might bring to your bank balance.

Changing Times

My involvement with journalists in emerging economies such as those of Kosovo, Bosnia, Lithuania, and Romania has broadly been an enjoyable and fruitful one. Most young journalists have a thirst for the profession but are often held back from maturing professionally by a system that developed under authoritarian rule and certainly didn't encourage original thought or enterprise stories. Protocol reporting is such an embedded mindset that most veteran journalists are mentally blocked with engaging in real journalism: asking questions, probing for answers, and not taking what they were told as fact.

Fortunately, for both journalists and the readers and viewers who follow them, times are changing. Reporters are beginning to ask questions. The fear of government or establishment punishments (especially losing a job) are lessening, and a more positive approach to tough questioning and serious writing is gaining strength as time goes by.

Freedom of the Media and Responsible Reporting

Journalists talk constantly about a free press while frequently omitting equal emphasis on the notion that freedom of the press must go hand in hand with responsible reporting. This is particularly so in emerging democracies such as the Balkans, South Caucasus, and CIS—but not exclusively so.

Because of the *News of the World* phone-hacking scandal in the UK, the government set up a government inquiry into how the press was regulated (Chapter 22). In fact, UK printed media until then had no statutory regulations but was governed by a voluntary system known as the Press Complaints Commission, a self-regulating body. The result was that for the first time in 200 years, UK media is now subject to terms listed in a royal charter, which has a committee that will act as auditor for a revamped regulatory system.

Because illegal and probably immoral means had been used to access information by phone hacking, stories using information from this practice by leading media organizations compromised freedoms previously enjoyed by the British press. As a result, reporters' activities will now be limited in scope. Hence, freedom of the media was eroded by irresponsible reporting from sections of UK journalists. This is a great loss to journalism everywhere, because Western governments have spent a great deal of cash helping revamp media regulations in countries that essentially controlled the press by government edict.

Most Western journalists have completed a university degree or recognized journalists' training course; but in many maturing democracies, qualifications or practical experience are not required, and a journalist is simply someone who decides to call himself or herself a journalist. This has in many cases limited the understanding of media responsibility among practicing third-world journalists.

It is understandable that there is euphoria among journalists who for decades have labored in a tightly controlled media at being let off the leash. But the result, at least initially, was a group of "reporters" who thought they were able to say anything about anybody without any facts to back up their stories.

Codes of Conduct in Emerging Democracies

It is important that all journalists—from countries with a strong tradition of a free media as well as those where democracy is a new concept—try to follow the voluntary local code of conduct set up by journalists for the industry and to familiarize themselves with government media legislation: what it includes and what they think as professionals it should include. Constantly review the impact these rules and regulations have on relations you as a reporter have with government and industry.

As a journalist, you should challenge the authorities if regulations make good governance of text and electronic media difficult in an emerging democracy. First, challenge regulation privately; then, if you have to, do it openly and publicly—not necessarily as an individual but through a professional association or journalists' club.

Some of the key elements in most journalists' codes of conduct cover issues such as the following:

- Don't bribe or take a bribe.
- Don't let politicians, businesspeople, public relations officers, or spin doctors play confidence tricks on you.
- Don't allow yourself to be coerced.

- If your story isn't honest, it's no good to anyone.
- Never, never allow pressure to be put on you because someone claims they know the owner of your newspaper or broadcast station.

Always ask yourself if you are doing the following:

- Paying attention to accuracy
- Making provision for a fair opportunity to reply
- Recognizing privacy issues
- Avoiding any form of discrimination
- Protecting your sources
- Not taking personal advantage of privileged knowledge and observing impartiality (especially important for financial journalists!)

A Test of "Real" Journalism

One journalist in a country that had been in the grip of a dictator told me of the hilarious situation she found herself in when she challenged the status quo and actually tried a little investigative reporting. For her efforts she was fired.

Crestfallen, she left the newspaper building and set off for home.

The next day she received a message that she needed to speak to the managing editor (a Western term … in communist times, no such post existed). She returned to the newspaper offices to find a straight-faced editor telling her (not asking her) that she was to resume her position as a reporter.

It appeared that when she was hired, no proper check had been made on her background. As such, no one had discovered that she was not a card-carrying member of the Communist party, which was a requirement for employment.

When senior staff had discovered that they shouldn't have hired her in the first place, they panicked because their jobs were on the line if it was discovered she had been hired illegally. So they told her to go back to her desk and resume her duties and not to tell anyone that she had been dismissed. That way, everyone kept their jobs. She carried on with her work, unencumbered with the fear of losing her job (she couldn't be fired), and, as a result, when the regime fell, she found herself with an extraordinary reputation as a good reporter. As of this writing, she is still one of her country's leading journalists.

But the fact remains that protocol journalism has stuck and unfortunately can still be found in many countries where democracy has developed green shoots and journalists are reveling in newfound freedom.

But never mind the emerging democracies: journalistic Luddites can still be found in Western societies.

Embracing Change

When trade unions held enormous power in the UK media of the '70s and early '80s, change came very slowly, and many in the industry refused to accept that change was on the way. If nothing else, technology was beginning to have an impact on journalism, changing the way in which reporters, editors, and news crews needed to operate. A small example was the way that news was covered for television. Film was still the order of the day in the UK and news crews could sometimes be counted in double figures just to bring a single item to a bulletin.

In Vancouver in the mid-'60s, I worked as a producer/reporter with only a cameraman and soundman/driver covering several items in a day with a camera, a microphone, and a 2-inch videotape machine in something that resembled a suitcase. Yet in the early '80s in the UK, such versatility was often denied a reporter. And well into '00s, archaic practices were still prevalent in much of the old Eastern Europe, Balkans, Baltics, and CIS.

The point about all this is that journalists, especially business journalists, must open their minds to change: embrace it, mold it to their own particular means of working, and understand the changes that are taking place on almost a daily basis around them.

When trying to enter into serious debate about change, the plaintiff cry can still be heard:

"But it won't happen to us!"

"What won't happen?"

"Change of course."

It's amazing how many journalists in countries across the globe take this view.

I am the first to accept that we have all only recently left behind a world where things were vastly different. But social upheaval and a revolution in technology have sent us rushing down a road to conformity that has left us breathless.

■ **Caution** Journalists who refuse to accept change—both that which has already occurred and that which is on the way—will be swept aside by it.

Sometimes change isn't that obvious, and that's when it is all too easy to fall into the trap of thinking it won't happen—or at least that it won't happen to me.

The Changing World of 24-Hour News

Jim Boulden is a familiar figure on CNN screens and a very able business reporter (Chapter 11). I worked with him at Reuters on the American PBS business programs *Morning Business Report* and *Nightly Business Report*, which were daily half-hour shows broadcast on PBS affiliates coast to coast in the United States. Feeling a bit inhibited with the restrictions that half-hour programs imposed on reporting styles, Jim switched his allegiance to CNN.

As most journalists do, I meet up with former colleagues who are also mostly old friends, and eventually the conversation turns from the old days to the new days. Jim and I recently sat in a good old-fashioned English pub, second home to many journalists, to swap stories over a pint.

It has been a few years since I have worked in a 24-hour news enterprise, and I was intrigued with what Jim told me about working at CNN. Many of the routines were familiar. Some things hadn't changed that much. But Jim pointed out the subtle shift of 24-hour news channels over just a few brief years.

Here's what he had to say about CNN's daily routine.

It used to be the case that news output had a 20-minute window that high-lighted the day's events, mostly in an evening newscast. It was known as a *revolving news wheel*.

That is no longer the case. A 24-hour rolling international news wheel is an outdated model. Now, the news that is broadcast in any given 24-hour period is broken up to bring *appointment viewing* to certain times of the day.

It's generally believed in news circles, and is backed up by research, that few people watch more than about 20 minutes of 24-hour news broadcasts in any one sitting.

Not so long ago, the concept was to simply repeat the same news every 30 minutes. But advertisers didn't like it. And viewers who did tune in and out throughout the day found it too repetitive. Frankly, those who worked on it found it boring and unmotivating. Simple—but boring and for the lazy.

▨ **Note**   The dirty word in 24- hour news nowadays is "dupe"—that is, to take the script from the last hour's rundown and move it over to the next hour.

So change took place, and that idea was replaced by a new concept, which was to neutralize broadcasting an hour's news. Anchors and reporters never said "Good morning" or "Good evening": the news sets never had a "morning" news scene and programs were no longer referred to as a "prime time" talk show.

Eventually, owners, managing editors, and above all producers and directors realized that this proved impractical and made for sterile news shows; people who work in news and those who watch the news, the all-important viewer, expect different things at various times of day and become consumers of them according to where they sit. The change in reporting techniques also made the job of a reporter more complex, so that a reporter could be expected to file a blog, a shorter version of a TV news package (in modern parlance these are called a "look-live" or "walk and talk"), as well as a 30-second explanatory piece called a "whip." So, one story may have to be told to an audience in three to four different ways.

But change, my dear fellow, is part of all our lives—and now there is an even newer concept, which is to keep writers, reporters, producers, and present-ers (anchors) working on the same part of the schedule each day, no rotation. The morning team in London is always the morning team. If you watch a chan-nel in the middle of the night abroad, say while you are awake in a hotel in Singapore, you are likely to see the same anchor or anchors, whether based in London or New York or those just waking up in the Hong Kong bureau.

So, the modern answer to the age-old question of who these days decides what news to cover—and how—changes from hour to hour and from show team to show team.

This is a new concept. It means internal competition between news teams for limited resources (camera crews, video editors, and other human and technical facilities), and it means that when breaking news trumps all other news items, everything else in the news program is thrown out of the window, despite hours of work put into a show before the "crisis" news was known about. When the breaking news of a financial crisis crashes into a newsroom, chess championships have no chance of airing. The days of simply repeating news until a big story breaks are long over when it comes to a 24-hours news wheel.

Change has made these all-news stations (and there are now a plethora of 24-hour news outfits) proactive in deciding what and how news is selected for broadcast and how to please an audience that only wants to watch for 20 minutes a day.

As we downed our last pint of beer and departed from the pub into the night, both Jim Boulden and I agreed on one thing:

The business news sector is full of contradictions.

Everything can be challenged. For every rule there is almost always an exception. The key to controlling successful news and information output is opening the mind and challenging the absolute. So, as Jim Boulden has come to accept, change is now swift but subtle, with adverse consequences for those who ignore it.

Key Points

- Ethics are the written and unwritten codes of moral standards that are critical to activities and aspirations of a business organization, including news media.

- Big business and financial institutions are not above applying pressure on journalists to turn a blind eye to some practices that might not be in the public good.

- Biased reporting can easily put a company out of business; this principle is exceptionally important in business news.

- Many journalists in emerging economies talk about a free press but rarely grant that freedom of the press must go hand in hand with responsible reporting.

- It is important that all journalists, from countries with a strong tradition of a free media and those where democracy is a new concept, try follow the voluntary local code of conduct.

- The days of 24-hours news wheels simply repeating news until a big story breaks are long over.

Making Economic Reporting Relevant

Headline: "Auto Industry in Crisis after Huge Worker Layoffs at …"

Once, not so long ago, even a dramatic story such as this would have been relegated to an inside page of a newspaper.

Now, business and economic headlines are the order of the day. Barely a day goes by when the headline news isn't related to business or the economy. People want and need to know about pensions, asset values, shares, fluctuating house prices, and other key issues of daily life:

- Are our jobs safe?

- Are taxes about to go up?

- Will savings produce real dividends?

Business and economic reporting is now meat and drink to media enterprises; such is the impact it has on ordinary lives, especially in a society where wealth is increasing, even at a slow pace. Economic reporting is more relevant than ever.

Defining What It Means to Be a Business Journalist

There are three main branches of business journalism: business, economic, and financial.

The term *business journalist* has become the "catchall" term for reporters covering all three of these types of reporting because the business journalist reports on economic change in a nation as well as reporting about major players such as CEOs, brokers, bankers, and other important individuals in the business world.

Economic journalists cover a more specific type of story within business, such as indicators of inflation, unemployment, interest rates, and consumer spending. From the indicators, expert analysts will forecast what is likely to happen to an economy such as recession or expansion. Economic journalists cover these predictions as well.

Financial journalists tend to focus on banking, treasuries, currencies, and the financial systems of a nation.

But as with most professions, drawing a definite line between these types of reporting is near impossible. Many business journalists cover all three.

So before we get into the real meat of this chapter, and to be clear, business journalism, according to Wikipedia, is "the branch of journalism that tracks, records, analyzes, and interprets the economic changes that take place in a society" and is used to describe coverage of financial and economic events as well.

This form of journalism is really no different from standard journalism in that it covers news and features and produces articles or stories about people and places. But business journalism focuses on issues related to the field of business. Today, because of its relevance, most newspapers, magazines, radio, and television news shows carry a business segment.

A business journalist reports detailed and in-depth business news disseminated through all types of mass media, including print and digital publications and radio and television channels, and dedicated specifically to business and finance events, trends, data, socioeconomic consequences, and profiles of major players.

Business and economic journalism is a serious business. You have to know what you are writing about, which documents to look for, and which sources to use; and you need to know the appropriate place to look for the information to make the story. While understanding the basic principles of economics, a business reporter must above all instill the discipline of asking for information.

Business reporters are not economists, analysts, or market makers. They are reporters. And although it is helpful to have an understanding that business is about a company's profits, the importance of the stock market, and a business's future prospects, asking the real experts is the most important factor.

Why Business Journalism Is Relevant to Journalists

There are two matters to consider in the relevance of business events. One is the relevance of business and economic reporting to journalists and the other is the importance of business operations to the average citizen.

Considering the few examples at the beginning of this chapter, it becomes evident that there is much business news for modern journalists to report, much more even than just 15 years ago.

The amount of financial information available to journalists has grown as the Internet has grown and business newswire services such as Reuters and Dow Jones have expanded. Added to these phenomena is the rise of the business news channels such as Bloomberg and CNBC, which in turn has pressured newspapers to pay more attention to business news.

The financial institutions themselves also now demand information on what's happening in the business and financial sector. It is impossible for bank and market analysts and stockbrokers to rely solely on their contacts and in-house information centers. They need to know what is happening and they need to know what the competition is saying in analyzing a set of financial circumstances—and they need to know it now.

The globalization of business and commerce has also been a force in the development of business TV and newswire services. Banks, brokers, businesses, and financial institutions can't cover everything that is occurring abroad. So the reliance by the financial sector on news organizations, which have the means of gathering the news, has become a key factor in the development of business journalism.

All these trends have led to changes in the way financial journalism is produced, and some of the major changes are addressed in different chapters of this book. Therefore, business journalism is relevant to those who want to disseminate important information to a wide congregation of society; and the content of business stories is important to almost everyone. Business, economics, and finance affect almost all our lives.

Why Business Journalism Is Relevant to Industry

Unless a business is listed on the stock exchange, it doesn't have to tell you what its net profits or net losses are. But it is generally in a company's interests to do so. Revealing this data can squash rumors that it is in trouble, can demonstrate that it is a company worth investing in or doing business with.

Losses don't mean that it is a company destined for the scrap heap. There are a hundred reasons why a company can make losses in a certain period but still be a very healthy business. For instance, it might have restructured and made part of the workforce redundant. That could have been costly in terms of severance pay but given it a bright future because it has become more efficient as a result of that move. Nevertheless, in that particular year as a result of that particular cost, it could overall have shown losses or a reduction in profit.

■ **Note** I have mentioned that accuracy is a very important feature of business journalism and good business journalists will take that diktat on board and use it in their arsenal of weapons in reporting credible stories.

It is necessary therefore to try and get a proper picture of a company's progress, and comparisons should be made over a similar period. For example, it might be necessary to compare revenues for one year against revenues for the previous year, or for a given quarter of one year against the same quarter of the previous year.

You should also try to determine what caused profit or loss in a particular company. Extra profits might come from expanding markets in a given sector, or losses might have come from a major fire at the plant. Explaining how a company has performed is part of the business journalists' job.

Why should any business give out this sort of information when it doesn't have to?

The business that is secretive will find it much harder to attract investment, partnerships, or even new customers. As more and more investment comes into a region, whether from other parts of the country or from overseas, businesspeople will be forced to become more transparent about their activities or face the possibility of serious consequences.

Why Business Journalism Is Relevant to Society

The following observations are made to illustrate how important research, accuracy, and facts are in making business news relevant to "society."

There is a prevailing belief that outside investment means someone puts cash into a business and then leaves it alone to get on with things. It would be wonderful if that was the way things worked. There are many businessmen across Eastern and Central Europe rubbing their bruises because they believed that this was so, or that their governments would make it so.

Inward investment comes in a number of ways. There are investors who will place their cash in a company simply to see a profitable return. But they need to be convinced that the company is a first-class company, efficient, capable, and handling its finances properly before risking their capital. Much of what they learn in the initial stages comes from what they read in the press. They read what journalists write. If a company hid behind its doors and refused to let media have a peek inside, then its chances of attracting the "docile" investor are nil.

Investment might come from a partnership, where an outside company wants to participate with an existing company. This is not uncommon, but these sorts of investments come because the local company has shown it is a worthwhile enterprise as a profitable partnership. Yes, of course such investors will want to see accounts and trading statements and a host of other documents before making a decision. But generally, they will want to see what position and image the company has in its market, and that comes from the sort of information that the business journalist has been reporting.

■ **Note**   Reluctance on the part of management to deal with business media might not be as big a hurdle as you think. There is a lot at stake for existing businesses in considering their future. Building knowledge about their activities in the community will play no small part.

Finally, there are outside investors who decide to opt for a "green field" situation. In other words, they will set up in competition with existing businesses on their own.

This is the very basis of the open market economy and usually results in winners and losers. The local business that has failed to explain its activities to its suppliers, customers, work force, bankers, and a whole host of other interested parties is likely to find a defense of its territory a lot more difficult than if it had won the confidence and respect of those people, before it faced competition.

A "Liquid" Example

I live in a small community some fifty miles south of London called Lewes. It has a brewery in the town, which was established in 1784. It has always been open with the local community, the local and regional media, and with other businesses.

A "LIQUID" LUNCH

There is an interesting divide between American and British journalists that is important to be aware of if you are a US reporter working in the UK or a British journalist operating in the United States. If there is alcohol served at a press conference, US journalists will usually stay away. If there is no alcohol at a press conference, then the Brits stay away. There is some substance to this notion, but of course, neither instance is set in stone! But the UK version is known as a "liquid" lunch (more booze than food).

The European beer industry has been subject to takeovers, amalgamations, and mergers. Yet this small brewery in Lewes has managed to fight off every big brewer that has tried to take it over. Because it has been so open and has won the community's respect, beer drinkers are loyal to its brand of beer.

Competitors have tried to ban this beer from its bars to put the brewery out of business. But the exact opposite has happened. Loyal customers refuse to drink in bars where this beer is not served. So the competitor is the business that is suffering, not the local business itself.

This is a direct result of the brewery being open with the media, open with the customer, and open with its community.

It is also a by-product of good business reporting that accurately gave the facts about this business to a public dependent on it for jobs, community support, a thriving industry, and faith in the marketplace.

Business news is relevant to people, and business reporting is relevant to that relevance.

More Breadth and Depth

Readers and viewers need help in understanding how business affects them, and there is no better way than seeing business news simply but accurately explained on TV, radio, or in newspapers by trained reporters who know how to tell a story.

So there is more breadth and depth required in business reporting than in general news to maintain a good level of understanding among an audience that increasingly demands to know what is happening with a country's economy.

Issues such as salaries, job security, interest on savings accounts, cost of living, and the price of goods or services are on the minds of a large section of the population.

Despite having straightforward labels, most of these issues can be very complex, and it is the skilled business reporter who can ensure that readers and viewers understand clearly the issues involved.

Good coverage of business, financial, and economic issues is needed and that is a vital requirement of an open market society that journalism can provide.

Key Points

- The term *business journalist* has become the "catchall" term for reporters covering financial and economic as well as business reporting.

- Business journalism is relevant because business, economics, and finance affect almost all our lives.

- Businesspeople in emerging economies will be forced to become more transparent about their activities—or face serious consequences.

- Investors want to know about companies into which they want to put their money.

- Readers and viewers need help in understanding how business affects them.

Getting the Best from Press Conferences

Going to a press conference can either be a day off or some of the hardest work you will ever do.

Public relations (PR) departments don't often discriminate between a story that is important to the press and a story that is important to their chairman. They should but they don't, and it is sometimes difficult for an editor or TV assignment producer to determine how important the information presented at the conference will be from the words included in the invitation to attend.

If it's not important, enjoy the free food and drink. If it is important, then make sure you get every fact and nugget of information that you can. Fight hard to get a one-on-one interview with the company executive who gave the presentation at the conference; and if any information is missing from your take on the story, get solid promises from the PR representative that this will be provided post conference.

■ **Note** The relationship between PR practitioners and journalists is a fragile one. Often, PR people refer to journalists rather disparagingly as "hacks," while the journalists are equally dismissive of PR people with the term "flacks." But the fact is that one sector needs the other, and journalists could not provide comprehensive coverage of news if PR companies and departments didn't exist.

The Benefits of Press Conferences

The most popular way of imparting information to media is through a press conference. It is an occasion in which a company can ensure that its message is directed towards journalists in a straightforward way while providing good background material at the same time in the form of information sheets, video news releases, photographs, press packs, and other important information. Mostly, it can be carried out in a convivial atmosphere with refreshments showered on the "hacks" who are there.

Much of the material handed out can be very useful to a journalist, and the direct contact with an authoritative spokesperson gives credibility to the story a "hack" intends to write.

The downside, as suggested previously, is that PR people often get the level of importance of a story wrong, reporters are left feeling their time has been wasted, and editors fret that they have committed human and technical resources that could have been better used elsewhere.

AVOID PRECONCEIVED NOTIONS

Don't let any preconceived ideas lessen your opinion about the usefulness of press conferences.

On one occasion in Northern Ireland, the accounting firm of Coopers & Lybrand (forerunner of PricewaterhouseCoopers) unveiled a document in which they analyzed the economy of the Province as if it were a listed company.

One reporter returned to base, telling the news editor it was just an attempt to soften up the media. The editor wanted to know later on in the day why the story was blazoned as a front page headline in the evening newspaper.

Prejudice cost that reporter a major story.

Business journalists rarely find press conferences useless. Most major companies, governments, civil services, chambers of commerce, and other business-oriented organizations usually use this form of press liaison to release facts, figures, important decisions, trade deals, and a variety of other financial and economic news to media.

It is rare that such information is trivial. But business journalists must be alert to the importance of the information and understand the background to it to make full use of the vehicle as a useful and reliable source.

It is likely that business press conferences will include facts and figures about a company, the economy, or the financial well-being of an organization. Knowing how to interpret data (Chapter 19) is an essential skill for a business journalist.

The Role of Press Conferences

Press releases, press conferences, and one-on-one interviews are all standard procedures for a journalist to get information. But the press conference and the interview are always a battle of wits between the reporter and the disseminator of information.

Press conferences are typically held by a corporate public relations department, spokesperson's office, or commercial public relations consultancy for a business, the government, or other organization. The aim of the press conference is not only to inform the press but also for the organization to control the way that information is made public.

In many cases, press conferences are a straightforward means of providing information to journalists and thereby the public. However, there have been many cases in which governments and businesses have issued press statements to try and obscure much more important information that is damaging to them. There are also instances of public relations personnel issuing statements that seem reasonably important but that hide the really hard story in the body of the text. Again, this is a way to conceal damaging information while enabling a government or business to deny that it withheld a story. In other words, the information was made available, but the press should have searched for it.

An example of this kind of skullduggery was the internal memo of a British government press officer who e-mailed colleagues, "It's now a very good day to get out anything we want to bury." The cynicism of this ploy caused media and public outrage as the day in question was September 11, 2001 (9/11), following the attacks on the World Trade Center.

▓ **Tip**   The journalist, especially the business journalist, must be on the lookout for tricks and dodges when considering information that is provided for them during press conferences.

What the Journalist Needs to Know Going In

The first decision in covering the news from a press release is for the journalist to determine whether the story is important enough for a press conference. Could it have been handed out in a press release? What is it about the story that makes it important enough for the organization to hold a formal press conference? As already noted, this is often a question that editors struggle to answer.

A common mistake among media managers is to call a press conference for relatively unimportant news. It is even more common for journalists to go to such press conferences, wasting precious time and resources. But if a press conference is called and a reporter attends it, the second thing he or she must remember is that the conference is biased in favor of the people holding it. The journalist who decides to report on the press conference must write any subsequent story without bias.

As a journalist, you may find that you are not on the invitation list to a press conference because you have been critical of a government minister, CEO, or a company. That is the risk that a reporter runs if stories are direct and honest. But that doesn't mean you have to accept it. There are lots of other ways you can check out the story and get information you need to write a piece. For example, talk to trade unions in the case of a business, or the opposition in the case of government. Remember, if a government or business tries to avoid critical journalists by not including them, the result can be uninformed comment and a hostile press: not a result they especially want.

Attending the Press Conference

After you arrive at the press conference, it's important to look for any information packs. Ideally this should contain the speech to be made at the press conference, a background sheet on the organization, photographs, and biographical notes on the speaker. This material is often not made available; but where it is, it can be very useful in putting a story into context.

Next, establish if there is a space set aside for one-on-one interviews after the press conference. Observe the priority order set by the organization. TV and radio usually need to go first because of deadlines. Make sure you know the rules of the conference. How long is set aside for questions? Will there be chance for interviews afterward? Can a supplementary question be asked after the initial one?

Usually, just before the conclusion of the press conference, there will be a question-and-answer session for journalists to clarify any information or to ask additional questions. In doing so, the organizers will ask journalists to identify themselves and the publication or broadcaster they represent when asking a question. But if they don't, do it that way anyway—and always stand up to ask your question.

Don't be afraid to ask direct questions. Journalists have been invited to attend and therefore the organizers have demonstrated their willingness to be cross-examined. But don't be rude or aggressive: firm is quite sufficient. Watch out for the spokesperson who tries to brush off your question by suggesting it is silly or not worth consideration. This is an old trick and is usually a way of not answering a question they don't want to answer. Insist on a reply.

If the spokesperson honestly can't immediately answer a question, insist that they supply the information requested as soon as they can. Follow up and make sure you get your answer later from the speaker or another staff member from the organization giving the press conference.

Tip If for a good reason you can't attend the conference, request a phone interview, or at the very least ask for the content to be sent to you either in press release or speech form. But don't be offended if the organizers won't provide material until after the press conference is over. It's only fair they give priority to those who attended.

Finally, try not to let spokespersons close the conference before all reasonable questions have been answered. Another favorite trick of organizers is to answer a couple of questions from "tame" journalists—that is, reporters sympathetic to the organization—then refuse to take other questions. They invited you, so there is no reason for you to accept such treatment.

If you happen to know the speaker, don't let him or her patronize you into being soft on them. It's the oldest trick in the world for a politician to walk into a room and speak a few words to reporters they know: "How's your wife? Good to see you again." It's a trick. Don't fall for it.

Do the job your editor has sent you to do.

A CASE OF PRESS CONFERENCE "TRICKS"

I was running a course for journalists in Armenia, where often young reporters are overawed by the fact that someone at a press conference is an important politician.

In this case, we had the minister of finance who had agreed to come to the course to be interviewed. In fact, the Ministry had made the rather silly comment previously that Armenia was totally unaffected by the financial crisis swirling around the rest of the world, so his presence was very pertinent to topical business stories.

I had warned the young journalists of the trick politicians use in "buttering them up" by picking on one or two of them to be familiar with and take the edge off any serious questions. And even if I had paid the guest to behave in that way, I couldn't have persuaded him to give a better demonstration of what I had warned my fellow journalists about.

The minister of finance entered the room, immediately spotted a face he recognized, and stopped and had a "friendly chat" before taking his place at the head of table. There was a nervous giggle around the room as the journalists recognized the trick he was using.

It gave them confidence to start to ask searching questions about the country's economy, and they began to perform in a way that was new and novel to them. And they got a good story from their endeavors because they managed to get an admission that overseas aid was likely to be reduced because of the financial crisis, thus putting the squeeze on the national budget.

At one point, the politician tried to divert attention by recalling a press trip he had had with one or two of the reporters. He failed to answer a question by diverting the conversation to the excellent lunch on the trip.

But by this time, the participants were alert to his ploy and, once they got their teeth in, didn't let go. The result was a slightly chastened minister and a much more confident press corp.

After the Press Conference

If the speaker circulates after the formal press conference's proceedings are over, watch out for denials in casual conversation. Nothing is ever "off the record" and "no comment" is unacceptable. Even if you are a text journalist, use a voice recorder to note all questions and answers. If you are challenged later for inaccurate reporting, it is a great safeguard.

Also, never tell the organizers what you are going to print or broadcast. This is your job, not theirs; and anyway, the best reporters will take time to think carefully about the angle they will choose.

Press Briefings

A press briefing is a different situation altogether. This is a way for organizations to chat with reporters about what the company or government department does and to provide the background for spot news, such as that emanating from a press conference. Briefings can be organized for a single journalist or for a group. Many reporters discount briefings because they take up nonproductive time. But they do put organizations and issues into context, so reportage is more accurate and demonstrates a good understanding of the issues.

Briefings can provide much greater understanding about an organization so that reporters look and sound as if they know what they are talking about. Some journalists sniff at this sort of attention to detail. But never discount the intelligence of your readers or listeners. They can be very perceptive, and they know when a reporter is trying to cover the fact that he or she doesn't really have much information about the story (or in fact doesn't know much about the issue).

Time spent at briefings can help a reporter's credibility and is time worth spending when an invitation to a briefing is received. People being questioned at a press conference sometimes complain what they say is "taken out of context" by reporters in any subsequent story. A press briefing gives the spokesperson a chance to give that context. At the briefing, guidelines should be set as to what or what cannot be reported, but as a rule direct quotes from the event should not be used.

As seasoned reporters know, there are two sides to every story. No matter how plausible the argument is presented at either a press briefing or a press conference, good reporters will examine the information carefully. Knowledge of the subject is very helpful because if there are gaps in the information being provided or something "doesn't sound right," then it becomes obvious some checking needs to be done.

■ **Term of art**   References to "protocol journalism" are scattered throughout this book. Protocol journalism is the practice of reporting, verbatim, information supplied in press release form or at a press conference without questions being asked. Protocol journalism should be avoided.

Ask as many questions as are allowed at a press conference, but ask as many if necessary after you get back to base to write the story. If it's a trade story, what do unions have to say? If the news is from a government, what do opposition politicians have to say? If it is an economic story, how does this fit in with an analyst's point of view? Keep on asking people on "the other side" of the story until you are satisfied that your news item is correct.

And don't let company officials off the hook. If they promised you to get additional information that was not available at the time of the conference, press them for it. Being a "terrier" is all part of being a journalist; being a bulldog gives that extra "bite" to a business journalist.

Key Points

- Identify yourself when asking questions at a press conference.

- Don't let speakers or company executives patronize you into not asking tough questions.

- Don't take "off the record" comments or accept "no comment" as a response.

Television Reporting Skills

I teach and train journalists from a wide variety of different overseas locations and, in the process, I learn a great deal about conditions in their own countries.

For example, Internet penetration is not extensive in many emerging economies, which is especially true of nations in Africa with large rural areas, such as Nigeria, with almost 170 million people scattered over a vast landscape. In Nigeria, 28 percent of the population uses the Internet. Bucking the world trend, newspaper circulation in Nigeria has increased substantially in a decade to 25 percent. But television coverage is more than 80 percent.

Information dissemination in many other emerging democracies throughout the developing world reflects a similar picture. Television is still an important means of getting news and information.

Nor should the Western world think that TV is becoming less important in developed nations because of the inroads being made by the Internet. TV producers, journalists, and broadcasters are "content" providers. Whether the audience chooses to watch on a conventional television service, a computer, iPad, or phone, the basic product is television.

The Visual Nature of Television

Television is a visual medium. Reporters must always give priority to the pictures, a skill known as "writing to pictures." The script should not say what is obvious. If the pictures show workers walking down the street chanting slogans, for example, it's both repetitive and foolish to say, "Strikers walked down the streets chanting slogans."

Instead, the words a journalist uses should give information not evident in the pictures. Continuing the same example, the reporter might say, "Five hundred people took part in a demonstration protesting redundancies at the car factory. This is the sixth consecutive day that workers have taken to the streets."

When reporting for television, detail should be kept to a minimum. Don't overwrite, and let the pictures breathe. This is especially important if there is some good natural sound on the tape: for example, the clanging of the bell at the New York Stock Exchange. Don't drown out the good natural sound with an endless commentary, and take pauses while reading.

Finally, as with any form of news writing, television reporters should write in short, simple sentences, avoiding long titles of people or organizations, which can be put on the screen as captions.

Tip   As with any reporting, give your viewer some credit. Never underestimate the intelligence of the audience. But never overestimate their knowledge either.

Keys to Successful Interviewing

Before doing an interview it is very important to research the subject thoroughly and, if you are able, to choose an interviewee carefully. Look for an interviewee who can speak clearly, concisely, and with authority.

An interview should be to the point; it should not be long and rambling, particularly for news items. The journalist should always be in control. The reporter decides how the room will be set up, decides where the interviewee will sit or stand, and, most importantly, determines the agenda of the interview and the questions.

LOSING CONTROL OF THE INTERVIEW

A very experienced and famous American interviewer Barbara Walters lost her focus on one occasion while interviewing actress Katherine Hepburn. Letting her mind wander and failing to concentrate on the interview, she asked Hepburn what kind of tree she would like to be. Hepburn answered she hoped she was not an elm, with Dutch elm disease. Walters admitted later that she was in a pickle with the interview but with good humor said that she, as the interviewer, "couldn't get out from under the branches." Nonetheless, it was far from professional.

There is only one important question in any interview and that's the first one. Thereafter, an interviewer must listen to the answer carefully before posing the next question.

It is always painfully obvious when an interviewer is reading prepared questions and downright silly when they get an answer to which their next question makes no sense.

> "Did you enjoy yourself last evening?"

> "No."

> "So which part did you especially enjoy?" Great interviewing!

Also, do not give an interviewee the exact questions in advance. You may perhaps tell them the first question in detail, followed by the general areas you want to cover. But if they know precisely what you intend to ask, they will rehearse the answers in their heads and their replies may sound stilted and "false" on camera, possibly even wrecking the credibility of your story.

Setting Up the Shot

Even if you only have five minutes available, thinking through a shoot and planning it is important. Don't assume that the cameraperson will cover every eventuality and remember everything for you. Work as a team.

Here are several key points to remember:

- Remind the camera crew to use a tripod if you need one, and to check on batteries, lights, and so on.

- Think about what setup shots you will need to establish the story.

- Once inside the building, look at the layout of the room and see where it is best to put the camera.

- At press conferences always get cutaways of other people reacting to the speaker.

- If possible try to influence how the shoot will take place, where the interviewee will sit, whether he or she is looking camera left or camera right, and so on.

- Listen for extraneous noise. Ask for radios, telephones, and so on to be shut off if they are likely to interrupt the interview.

In single interviews, always try to get extra shots that can be used as cutaways or illustration: for example, a picture on the desk or the interviewee's hands.

■ **Tip** Plan for the expected ... so you can cope with the unexpected.

When the viewer sees an interview, it often looks as if there were a number of cameras recording the event. But two-camera shoots are rare. A reporter usually has to make do with a single camera.

To make sure that the report moves along in sequence, a few actions are required to give that impression. The camera needs to be moved so that the interviewer can be seen asking questions of the interviewee. A couple of "two shots" help the look of the event—that is, when interviewer and interviewee are both seen in the shot.

This means the person being interviewed has to wait around for a few minutes after the camera has ceased recording the actual interview. Most business leaders and politicians are quite used to this and readily stay for those few extra minutes. If someone is in a bit of a rush or not used to being interviewed for TV, it's still possible to make the "package" look attractive. Generally, though, if the requirement is patiently explained, most interviewees will stay behind.

The reporter and camera crew must work on a few extra items immediately after the interview:

- For reverses/cutaways/*noddies* (those silly moments when the interviewer nods blankly at the camera), keep the camera close to the interviewee.

- For mute noddies, the reporter must look interested, perhaps nodding his/her head slightly (but not too much).

- If time is short, the reporter can move into the chair or position previously occupied by the interviewee; but the reporter must make sure that he or she is looking in the opposite direction to the guest and that the background is different.

- Remember the risk of "crossing the line." The camera must stay on the same "side" as it was when facing the interviewee after being moved to record questions from the reporter. Otherwise, the two people will end up looking away from one another rather than at one another.

- If you have two cameras, you should cross-shoot, remembering not to "cross the line," so the camera positions need to be on the same side of the reporter and interviewee.

- Try to match the shots so you have similarly sized shots to cut together.

- Be careful of objects on the set. The same thing should not be included in the shot of the interviewee and then in a reverse as they will appear to "jump" across the room.

- Even the most seasoned reporters sometimes forget they have a microphone attached to them. Be careful you make no comments you really should keep to yourself. The world may hear them. As microphones are sometimes attached to the camera, the cord will either strangle you as you move away, or more likely you will bring all the technical gear crashing down.

All of this activity is known as the "shoot," whether it is done inside a building or outside in the open air. The shoot provides the skeleton of the item to be broadcast, and it is now the responsibility of the reporter, sometimes with the aid of a video editor, to flesh out the item to make it a proper picture story and an attractive news presentation.

Then, back at base, the reporter has to begin a new sequence of events to produce a complete and polished video story.

Writing and Recording the Story

Introductions are normally written by the journalist who has worked on the story and then adapted by the presenter. Writers must ask

- Is the introduction clear and easy to follow?

- Does the introduction tease the viewers, leaving them with an urge to watch the report?

- Will the viewer understand the content?

- Does it contain irrelevant rubbish?

- Is the story told up front or has it been buried in the report?

Once the report is written, check that

- you can read it easily when recording

- the viewer will understand it

- you covered the key elements of the story

And once the report has been recorded, check the following:

- Did you fluff your words? Should you record it again?
- Did you read the story at a pace that the viewer could understand?
- Did you read the story with authority?
- Were you just "reading" the words—or communicating them to the viewer?
- Did you sound bored?

Sound recording tends to flatten the human voice, so it is often a good idea to put a little more emphasis into your voice. When recording a "light" or funny story, for example, you should hear a smile in the voice.

Note   Each writer will have a distinctive style; even so, a television journalist will have to adjust to the "house" style of the broadcaster. Most news organizations will have a house style guide so that journalists know both the writing and picture editing (cutting) style that is expected from the day they are employed. There is nothing more irritating for a viewer than to have news bulletins and business reports looking, sounding, and feeling different from day to day or hour to hour.

Editing the Interview

Reporters should not write a script for a complicated item or story and then simply plaster pictures over it to fit. This practice is one of the major causes of boring reports.

Before starting to edit (cut) the video, reporters need to assemble on paper a short cutting script based loosely on what they know they want to say; which bits of the interviews are to be used, and a list of pictures that could be used to cover the points. This is the responsibility of reporters, but in most organizations, a video editor will assist in the process. These video editors are fondly known as "cutters" because, before videotape, part of the process involved actually cutting pieces of film and sticking them together. The name remained as part of TV folklore.

Modern journalists can and often do edit their story without technical help because computer software is available for them to do it. This is much more efficient, but I always valued the input of a video editor who saw the interview from a different perspective and could add valuable suggestions on making the edit attractive.

Usually, reporters write a draft script before starting the edit process. This gives them a chance to find suitable pictures. But as the story/interview is being cut, keep adjusting the script to help fit the available pictures and vice versa. When—but only when—you are satisfied that it all works and makes sense, you can record the commentary.

▓ **Note**   There are, of course, many more skills to master, such as writing a script to exact time—three words per second is the rule of thumb—and building a sequence of shots to demonstrate an action. Such a sequence may be illustrated by the example of filming a golf player. The sequence would see a long shot of the golfer, a closer shot of his hands gripping the club and a shot of the backward swing, and a view of the ball on the tee before going back to seeing the ball shooting off down the fairway. If the basic tips outlined earlier in this chapter are followed, the rest will come as a journalist gains in experience.

The Making of a News Program

I have mentioned that I was the London anchor of the American daily, coast-to-coast, business program on PBS, *Morning Business Report*. My co-anchor in the United States was the very beautiful and very accomplished TV business journalist, Melissa Conti.

To make a TV program appealing, the presenters must "spark" off each other. There must be a mutual charisma, an appearance of liking each other, trusting each other, and admiring each other's professional abilities. This I enjoyed with Melissa and each morning, while waiting to go on the air, I would bounce up and down on the balls of my feet and create a huge beam on my face to try and match Melissa's bubbly personality. It worked well, and each morning I would open up the link with a very hearty, "Good Morning, Melissa!"

Our "set" was an open plan. The camera was located in the middle of the Reuters newsroom so the viewer could see Reuters' journalists working away in the background. It worked very well.

FUN IN THE NEWSROOM

One morning, the entire Reuters work force combined to play a prank on both of us.

As I said in front of the camera, "Good morning, Melissa!" the entire newsroom rose to its feet and echoed in chorus, "Good morning, Melissa!" It brought the house down, and it was a morning to remember because trying to broadcast serious business news after that was a tall order.

But this was an American program, and while the London anchor made important contributions, the guts of the news was generated in the United States.

To help readers understand how a program of this sort works, I asked Melissa if she would write the following brief description of *Morning Business Report*.

The Making of *Morning Business Report*
By Melissa Conti Winton

Beating the Billionaire

From 1979 to 2013, *Nightly Business Report* (NBR) was a dominant force in TV business news, airing on public stations throughout the United States. Produced at WPBT-TV, Channel 2, in Miami, Florida, NBR was the first in the nation to focus solely on news of the business and financial world. But in the early 1990s, financial information mogul Michael Bloomberg wanted to snatch that domination with the introduction of a short 15-minute morning business newscast.

The program with a talking anchor head, busy graphics, and lines of news scrawling at the bottom of the scene revolutionized the way TV business news was presented and it shook up the producers of NBR, who were already busy fighting off cable business news giant CNBC. Not only did Bloomberg's new program air on his financial terminals located in every major financial and brokerage house in the United States, it also started airing on various public television stations nationwide.

NBR saw this as a direct attack in their backyard and quickly created a new morning business news program to compete against the mogul turned mayor.

The KISS Staff

Without much funding and time, NBR chiefs brought the KISS journalism principle (Keep It Short and Simple) to a whole new level. With the purchase of a brand new nonlinear computer editing system, they were able to pull together a national television program with a very short staff of six: an anchor, who was also the producer and writer (and makeup artist and hairstylist); a director, who was also the technical director; an associate producer, who was also graphics producer (and general therapist to the anchor in times of high stress); a cameraman, who was also the editor and floor director; and two correspondents, one from Japan and the other from London. In 1994, *Morning Business Report* (MBR) was born and immediately sent to the frontlines in the fight for business news eyeballs. I was appointed the General.

Early to Rise (Very Early)

At first, it was flattering to be given the titles of anchor, producer, and writer (and supervisor) of a new morning business news show. But as anyone who's ever worked on morning television will tell you, those jobs come with a big price—the price of normal sleep. Even though we aired at 6 A.M. Monday through Friday, the *MBR* staff had to report to work at 2 A.M. because there was much to be done before I said "Good morning, I'm Melissa Conti" to public television viewers across the country.

Rising at 1:00 A.M. to get to work by 2 A.M. was exciting at first, given the novelty of the job, but as time wore on, it became clear to me that humans were definitely not meant to be nocturnal creatures. Regardless of the amount of sleep I was able to get during the day, I was perpetually tired and required increasing amounts of caffeine. After 9 years, I still wake up at 1 A.M.

Taking the Lead

My main goal when I walked in the station door at 2 A.M. was to make *MBR* as fresh as possible—to deliver the latest business and financial news and to explain to our target audience how that news might impact their investments and businesses. I sat down at my desk (wrapped my hair in curlers) and culled the Associated Press newswires and newspapers, namely, the *Wall Street Journal* and the *New York Times*, for the latest and greatest news and, at the same time, watched the early, early morning newscasts (as well as a bit of sumo wrestling on Japanese TV). I spent much time contemplating the lead story, which usually ended up to be about a major corporate merger or acquisition, a corporate bankruptcy, a major world event that would impact world financial markets, or, some days, all three.

Once I decided on the lead story, I ordered relevant video from the editor (who was usually sleeping in the back editing bay). I grabbed my Rolodex (for the young people reading this, we used to write phone numbers on paper cards attached to a round apparatus) and located a financial analyst who would comment live by phone on how the news in the lead story would impact financial markets.

World News from Japan and a British Bloke

Also enlisted in the battle for business viewers were two other television anchors from Reuters TV—Lucy Craft in Tokyo and Keith Hayes from London. Lucy's intense, get-to-the-point style of reporting was in sharp contrast to Keith's always jovial (except during tragic events) news delivery. Their task was to inform our viewers of the latest business and financial news in those areas of the world, including how their financial markets were trading, in light of their potential influence on Wall Street.

Their reports, usually five to seven minutes in length, were fed via satellite to our editor before *MBR* aired. Our skeleton crew and matching budget prevented us from going live with those reports at 6 A.M. Of course, today, with the advent of the Internet, budget and crew size would no longer be such an obstacle.

Numbers News

Another major component to our business and financial newscast was numbers. Reports released by the US government such as unemployment, housing, and inflation, as well as corporate earnings reports, had the potential to rally or repress Wall Street, so I made sure to include a segment on the reports expected that day and the often times unrealistic expectations of financial analysts. The numbers news was presented in a package by one of the *NBR* correspondents based in New York reading the upcoming numbers right to camera with graphics.

The Rundown

Once I decided on and assembled all the components in consultation with the director, associate producer, editor, and the overseas folks, it was time to populate the rundown. The almighty rundown is a TV tool that keeps everything that goes on air, be it news or entertainment, organized and within a certain time frame. It is essentially a list of items with a running time tally. Much like a puzzle, each piece of a newscast has to fit exactly into a certain time frame (and I mean down to the second, exactly).

Without the rundown, TV producers and directors would have no idea what comes first, next, or last and when to bring the anchor on camera, roll packaged reporter stories, video, graphics, and advertising (or *underwriting*, as we call it in the public television realm). The following is a sample of the *MBR* rundown with its running time tally in minutes and seconds. *MBR* was exactly 15 minutes in length.

Headlines Voice-Over (VO) to On Cam (Anchor is on camera) 0:30 0:30

Underwriting VO 1:00 1:30

Lead intro On Cam 0:10 1:40

Lead story Reporter package or VO or graphics 1:00 2:40

Tokyo intro On Cam 0:10 2:50

Tokyo segment Lucy Craft package 2:00 4:50

London intro On Cam 0:10 5:00

London segment Keith Hayes package 5:00 10:00

U.S. Equity Markets On Cam to Equities graphics 1:00 11:00

Commodities Markets Graphics w/music 0:20 11:20

Other Business News On Cam w/VO 1:00 12:20

Interview Intro On Cam 0:10 12:30

Long-Form Interview Roll video 1:00 13:30

General News Headlines On Cam w/VO 0:20 13:50

Business/Financial News Recap On Cam w/Graphics 0:30 14:20

Good-bye On Cam 0:10 14:30

Underwriting VO 0.30 15:00

And in 3, 2 …

Once the rundown was complete, I sent it off to the director, associate producer, and editor/camera guy. If there were no objections (and there usually weren't since I had a great crew that was able to perform the impossible every single day), I rushed off to the makeup room to perform the impossible— looking happy and awake at 6 A.M. in the morning. Because we had no money in the budget for a makeup artist and no makeup artists wanted to work for free at 5 A.M., I did my own.

By 5:30 A.M. (most days), I was ready and headed to the studio to make sure all was on track with the crew. I checked my microphone and IFB (a special earpiece that enabled me to hear the director) to make sure they were working. The editor/cameraman/lighting guy/floor manager checked all the equipment in studio. I checked the teleprompter, which I ran myself, and read through some of the scripts. I also checked the computer on the set to make sure there was no breaking news on the newswires, and finally, it was showtime. The director cued me "in 3, 2, 1" and *MBR* was on the air live at 6:00 A.M. Eastern time. (Public television stations had the option to air the show live or wait for other shows, which were fed continuously by satellite.) As the show was rolling live, I would often check the wires during reporter packages and interviews; and when breaking news occurred, I made the decision to roll the show again live at 6:15 A.M. through 6:30 A.M. The show was re-fed continuously until 8:00 A.M. Following a one-hour break, I would freshen the news and we went live again at 9:00 A.M. for stations on the West Coast.

Postscript   In 2001, the attacks on 9/11 left the country and the world shaken and sped up the erosion of the US economy and the eventual end of *Morning Business Report*. In 2002, computer giant Hewlett Packard ended its underwriting contract for *NBR*, thus stripping the morning show of the little budget it had. In October of 2002, the staff was informed that *MBR* would be cancelled at the end of the year.

Key Points

- Write your script to the pictures. Don't make the script ape what the pictures are showing.

- Check your voice-over. Be careful to avoid fluffs and mistakes and re-record if necessary.

- The most important question in an interview is the first one. All other questions and answers should follow on from that.

- Choose your pictures carefully. Poor selection makes a story boring and difficult to watch.

Reporting on Business for Television

There is a tendency to think of business reporting on TV as somehow separate and different from "ordinary" news reporting.

In the main this is simply not true. Just because channels like Bloomberg, and programs like BBC World News' "World Business Report" or those in CNBC's "World" global business news network have a distinctive style does not mean that they produce these programs—or individual reports within them—with different skills compared to straight news journalism.

The role of business television journalism needs to focus on how the journalist should gear his or her approach to the specific medium of television and electronic broadcasting. But before I get into that, let's talk about who watches business television.

Business Television Viewership

There are two distinct primary audiences of people who watch business programs. One is the upwardly mobile executive who has spare cash and wants to increase his or her capital. The other is the professional banker, broker, analyst, or economist. A secondary audience is the businesspeople who want to stay abreast of what is happening in their sector or what their competitors are up to. These primary and secondary audiences are considered to be "professional" viewers.

The main business television channels of the early "noughties," or 2000s, found a correlation in audience figures to the state of the economy. In the boom years of that decade, audiences soared. Because of an increase in personal income, younger people who worked in certain professions (such as lawyers, doctors, and architects) and who had never previously invested in stocks used extra funds to buy shares. These young professionals avidly watched markets and share prices and investment opportunities on television to increase their portfolios. Even more so, surveys found, they got a happy feeling from watching business news that reported their shareholdings prospering and their bank balances bulging.

Conversely, when economies contracted, the same professionals didn't want to hear that their shares were losing value and their assets were shrinking. So they stopped watching. Business journalists can't do much about that, but it is important to be aware that the business television viewing habits of individual amateur investors, especially those with modest shareholdings, are driven by the state of the economy. So viewership rises and falls in line with global economic fluctuations.

The professional viewer is quite different from the young professional or individual viewer. Brokers and dealers have TV sets at their desks (or at least on their computer screens) and watch avidly as anchors report the latest fluctuations in the financial markets. After all, business news is *their* business.

For the professional financial executives, TV business reporters must make sure that business television "adds value." These people who need the numbers (market movements, stock prices, and so forth) usually have this information at their desks. What they want from TV is comment and analysis. So the importance of guests in business television can't be understated.

TV business reporters can achieve a different dimension by focusing on the main things individuals, both professional financial people and small investors, want to know from a business story—which is primarily, "How do I make money out of this?"

Business Television: A Common Vision

Above all, journalists and producers need to be very astute about the type of guests they manage to persuade to appear on their shows.

Broadcasters, TV stations, and TV news operations differ both within countries and from country to country. But there is one thing they all have in common, and on which they all agree—the staff must all be aiming for the same thing and have a common set of editorial and visual standards to which they work.

In other words, the entire news staff—journalists, presenters, producers, reporters, subeditors, researchers, camera people, editors, sound people, graphics people, and so forth—must all share a common goal and, more importantly, they must all work to an agreed house "style"—a way of shooting, editing (cutting), writing, and so forth that is consistent across all news bulletins, day to day, week to week. This applies across all genres—business reporting, general news, and investigative and specialist reporting.

But each station, each program must create an identity so that viewers know without seeing the station logo that they are watching the program that provides them with the best information.

Obviously the choice of style and how an individual report—or even a whole program—looks will vary from station to station and is often dictated by what kind of audience (for example, what age group) the broadcaster is aiming at.

■ **Note**   In this chapter, I don't try and set out a style to be adopted but rather a few guidelines and rules that are the commonly accepted minimum standards to which any serious news (or business) reporter should aspire.

Writing Stories for Television

Business reporting on television should be seen as an "extra dimension." To attract a viewer, the basic rules guiding competent television reporting need to be stringently observed by a business reporter. Best television practice should be the cornerstone on which the specific of business reporting is built.

As noted in the previous chapter, television is a visual medium. It may seem obvious, but it's often forgotten, particularly by people who move to television from print or radio. Reporters should always give priority to the pictures. Writing for business television needs to be supplemented by excellent graphics and technical wizardry, and the story running orders need extra special consideration.

Knowledge of business, economics, finance, and trade is essential to good business news reporting. In the early days of coming to grips with TV and some of its complications, such as creating a picture story and coloring the presentation with moving graphs and pie charts, non-broadcast journalists found it all too easy to forget the basics of journalism generally and basic TV journalism in particular.

It is therefore incumbent on any TV business journalist to approach the task of reporting on television by applying the basics religiously.

Don't abandon the basics of journalism. ALL stories should include what is sometimes called "5-W-H"—that is, What, Where, When, Who, Why, and How.

To elaborate

- What is happening?
- Where is it happening?
- When did it happen?
- Who is involved?
- Why is it happening?
- How has it come about?

ALL news stories should answer ALL these questions. Television news is no exception.

News has been described as "the first rough draft of history" and "the immediate, the important, the things that have an impact on our lives." This applies as much to business reporting as to "hard" news.

HARD VERSUS SOFT NEWS

News is generally categorized as being hard or soft. This too applies to business news.

Hard news provides stories about events that have just happened or are about to happen. They are reported as an account of what happened, why it happened, and how the viewers are affected.

Soft news produces stories that are intended to entertain or inform. There is often an emphasis on human interest or a novelty factor. They may focus on people, places, or issues that affect the viewers' lives: for example, a new invention that the inventor hopes will make him or her a millionaire.

LONG-FORM BUSINESS PROGRAMS

We tend to think of business news in terms of short news items, but there is no reason that business cannot (and in fact does) feature in long-form current affairs programs or documentaries.

Even areas such as sports can be seen through "business" eyes. A London-based production company made a regular half-hour program called "The Business of Sport," which contained nothing but reports about the business side of sports. It was shown in dozens of countries around the globe.

Business Journalists Must Take Extra Care When Broadcasting

Business television news has a greater responsibility than regular news when it comes to credibility. People's money is at stake—tax money, wages, pensions, and a whole lot more. As a consequence, reporters should resist giving their own opinions in their news package but rely on experts. Therefore, having contacts among a whole range of experts who are willing to be interviewed is paramount.

And as such, it is usually necessary to have at least one video clip (sound bite) of an expert or interviewee in any business news package, sometimes two. The independent expert is vital to the credibility of business news items.

Where the audience is a specific one, such as bankers, businesspeople, traders, and so forth, television provides comment and analysis. This will be especially true as economies move from transitional to mature open markets.

It is best to get analysts and experts on camera or live in the studio; but where this is not possible, then the use of telephone interviews is completely acceptable, showing a photo of the expert or his place of work on screen.

If instead the audience is the ordinary man in the street, make sure there is plentiful use of graphics, charts, and tables. In this age of sophisticated graphic art, the graphics can move and jump and add to the overall compilation of an interesting and watchable piece of television. There are now "swipe screens" available where with one brush of the hand, pictures or graphics or text can be swiped onto or off an in-studio screen.

Be extra careful about "strap line" identification of any pictures of people you use. The Queen of England will not be amused if she is identified as First Lady Michelle Obama or vice versa.

A junior desk reporter will probably be given the task of writing brief headlines on any moving "ticker" that appears beneath the news program. Business journalists should check these ticker stories carefully. The slightest mistake (and because they are often written in a hurry, there are many) can have serious consequences if allowed to run unchanged.

TICKERS: GOOD OR BAD?

There is a sharp division between journalists over the use of tickers. Most business journalists approve of their use, especially for things such as market closing prices and foreign exchange rates. But many reporters believe they can be overused, so they clutter up the screen, making viewing a single story or even an entire business program difficult. The opposite argument is that such information is demanded by the professional viewer who wants detailed financial and economic data on his trading screen 24 hours a day.

Finally, when doing a piece to camera, try to make your sign-off as pertinent as possible to the story while putting a little action into the piece.

On one occasion I was reporting on a European potato shortage. During the piece, which was reported in Britain but targeted for an American audience, I made a slightly amusing comparison between the difference in meaning of some English words with their American counterparts such as cookie for biscuit, biscuit for scone, and crisp for chips.

In my piece to camera, I ate some french fries, called chips in the UK, while summing up my story. I reported on the fact that the staple English diet of fish and chips would become very expensive if the potato shortage lasted and at this point ate a "french fry," saying "So the staple diet of chips, excuse me, french fries, may disappear from UK menus."

Fairly simple "drama," but that clip is used by colleagues even today in training courses to demonstrate how to make a serious business story attractive and amusing.

Working as a Team

Sometimes it is necessary to do quick-fire reporting on the "hoof," such as the UK finance minister (known as "The Chancellor of the Exchequer") unveiling his annual budget to the House of Commons. No one but the senior members of government knows what the budget contains, so reporters have to pick the important points from the speech as it is being given.

This is where teamwork comes in, and for important business and economic information such as this, journalists should work in a team. It might be a team from your own TV station or it might be competing reporters from other media. I have often been in a press room when this sort of situation prevails, and to ensure that serious mistakes aren't made, I have worked closely with "competitors" to ensure my reportage was correct.

Television journalists should work closely with the producer, director, and technical personnel on a business news show. Working in cooperation on business journalism with colleagues and competitors is vital to successful reportage. Accuracy and the audience come first. Competition can sometimes take a back seat in the interests of the viewer.

Producing Successful Business Documentaries

There is an obvious difference between reporting "hard" business news and soft news and yet again between story reporting and documentaries.

Graham Addicott worked for many years as a business reporter for the London weekday TV company Thames Television. He then set up his own award winning and very successful documentary production company First Freedom.

Here, Addicott explains the philosophy about making business documentary programs from the background of having produced more than 50 acclaimed programs over a decade (and he is still doing so).

Addicott says that the secret to making an entertaining business documentary for mainstream television is to try and make it look as little about business as possible. "By which I don't mean that it can't be serious, or tackle a serious subject," he says. "But it should try to avoid duplicating the coverage done by normal business programmes, and channels like Bloomberg and CNBC."

An example follows: news might cover the World Islamic Economic Forum (WIEF) by concentrating on the speakers of the day, and current affairs coverage might take one of the debates and flesh out the subject. But a documentary has to try and find a different angle—following a delegate from his or her home country perhaps, or taking a look at the Halal Industry and weaving in any WIEF debates there might be as background to the main story line.

The business documentary should try to appeal to as wide an audience as possible but at the same time recognize that audiences differ from broadcaster to broadcaster (a documentary or series will be very different in tone and content on BBC World News to one on the Discovery Channel). So it is important when thinking of a subject to tackle, and of how to tackle it, to think of the audience: and also of the style of the broadcaster you will be making the program for—"There is no point trying to sell red shoes to someone determined to buy green ones."

All stories have a beginning, middle and end; but in the case of documentaries, the opening and closing sequences are perhaps the most important part of the whole program—these are the sequences that most people will remember, so they should be both visually and editorially strong. "Tell them you are going to tell them, tell them, and then tell them you have told them" is not a bad structure for a documentary.

■ **Note** The great advantage documentaries have over typical business news stories is time—time to construct arguments using the interviewees, time to allow pictures to "breathe," time to let the pictures and the interviewees tell the tale, and time for the audience to mull over what they are watching.

To that end shooting and editing has to be much more considered—it is not enough to write a script and just put wallpaper pictures over words and interviews. Everything about the documentary—pictures, commentary, and interviewees—has to blend into a whole. Planning is vital, as are reconnoitering locations, people, and picture shots (known as *recces*) for a documentary program.

Reporting on Business for Television

It is not boring to repeat the adage that Addicott used in explaining how to approach a business documentary; so read yet again: "Tell them you are going to tell them, tell them, and then tell them you have told them."

So here goes with a reminder about the key elements of reporting on business for television. And be sure to remember how the television journalist should gear his or her approach to the specific medium of television and electronic broadcasting.

Every business and financial reporter working in television must ask the vital questions "Why do people watch it?"and "What can it achieve?" The main thing people want to know from a business story is "How do I make money out of this?" So it is important that a reporter makes business television stories that offer "added value"; the professional audiences have the numbers, so they want comment and expert analysis; and the importance of guests in business television mustn't be underestimated. The good reporter will remember that a story is a story is a story; use the basics, of "who, what, where, when, why, and how," in making difficult and complex financial stories simple; and remember how to determine and address your audience.

Constantly examine the detail of what business television needs to communicate to a general public and determine the differences in approach for a business or economic audience: using commentators to back up the stories and where to get qualified people; the use of telephone interviews, the importance of asking the right questions; and understanding that views and sentiment drive markets and how that impacts on sources of guests and/or sources of news.

Remember that writing for business television isn't boring, so it's important to understand how to properly write and structure a business television story; keep in mind your colleagues needs and accept the importance of the introduction you must write for an anchor; and learn how to write a news package "off the intro" using a "grab (sound bite)" with a package and ascertain whether a story needs a guest.

Practice how to deal with structuring a news package on paper using interviews shot earlier, establishing what pictures are required and where they will come from, deciding how best to illustrate the story, and the importance of graphics and deciding if the story needs a graphic.

Nothing is set in stone: "The Golden Rule of Journalism is that there is no Golden Rule." Sounds familiar doesn't it? It is important that you make positive decisions but not be afraid of changing your mind.

Think carefully about how to assemble running orders, deciding if the interview should go live, and understanding why journalists talking to journalists on air doesn't usually work unless you are establishing a presence.

Many times you will have to deliver under pressure and be prepared if the program hits problems. Remember it is important to look after your guests, briefing presenters and handling breaking news. In other words, the good business journalist will be prepared to react to any given situation.

A VALUABLE LESSON

I remember when I first started in commercial radio. I was the cub, the newcomer, the neophyte.

I was completing the assembly of the 17:30 news bulletin one evening and feeling very cocky and proud at the job I had done when the senior shift journalist asked who had taken the wire copy from the shelf.

I confidently piped up that I had. He snatched the paper from my hand and growled that no one touched that except the senior who would read the 18:00 major bulletin.

I had 30 seconds to find some replacement news, so in desperation, I grabbed the first pieces of wire copy that I could. I then spent 5 minutes reading a news bulletin that consisted of a vivid description of the mating habits of the buffalo in Northern Manitoba. I can remember the sweat drops beginning to trickle down my nose the more I read of this enthralling story.

But the moral is I managed to do the newscast despite a very difficult situation, and I learned a valuable lesson on newsroom procedure the hard way!

A Bright Future for Television News

It might be a strange thing for a journalist to say that peace has been the driver of business news, when the very essence of a news story is based on conflict. But the cessation of global military conflict over almost three quarters of a century, and the collapse of many authoritarian governments, has made business reporting increasingly important.

Large numbers of countries in Europe, Asia, and Africa have started to develop open market economies. World trade is booming, despite the setbacks of occasional economic recession. Domestically, populations have seen wealth and living standards increasing; and more people have taken an interest in wealth-creating investments such as stocks and bonds.

All this has caused a steady shift of news emphasis in all media from death and destruction to reportage of business and economic news.

With the technological advances in communications such as Internet, satellites, micro TV cameras, and 24-hour news channels, TV business reporting has boomed and continues to do so.

The growth in business and economic news media has been strong and looks as if it will continue to be so. These are exciting times for reporters in the journalistic profession to become business reporters. In an industry that is hiring less staff, the number of business news reporters is on the increase; and with the exciting advances in the medium of TV, business news is a field that can set the pulse racing.

Key Points

- When economies are booming, audiences for business television increase. When a recession sets in, audiences for business TV decline.

- Staff working in business TV must have a common set of editorial and visual standards to which they work.

- Writing for business television needs to be supplemented by excellent graphics and technical wizardry.

- Differentiate between hard and soft news, but appreciate both are important.

- When producing a business documentary, think about the audience you are aiming at.

Newswire Agencies and Their Role

Newswire agencies, also known as *newswires*, are vitally important to business news journalists, whether they work for newspapers or electronic enterprises. Newswire agencies report on events, announcements, economic statistics, and other developments that are relevant to the markets.

Journalists at these organizations have to be extra-talented, extra-analytical, and above all extra-careful. They normally have a close relationship to business, government, politics, bankers, brokers, and other members of the broad economic community. This isn't just because they distribute news to thousands of news outlets and other entities such as banks themselves; it is also because both they and the business community need to be sure they get the information right.

ONE WORD CAN MAKE ALL THE DIFFERENCE

I once omitted one word from a report on a *Morning Business Report* bulletin. The story I filed said that the homes of executives of leading European plane maker Airbus had been raided across Europe in connection with some irregularities at the company.

The story went on TV at 0600 in the United States. By 0605, Airbus PR people were on the phone, angrily denying the story. I missed out one important word: "former." It was former executives whose homes had been raided. I was a very lucky reporter. The mistake, albeit small, was picked up by a professional viewer very quickly. We were able to correct the error in seconds.

But if the mistake had been about the company's shares, for instance, trading could have involved millions of dollars changing hands. I hold my hand up to this error, and indeed we all make them and will continue to make them. But accuracy is absolutely vital to newswire journalists because they send out thousands of bits of vital information on companies, stocks, banks, and prices; and one misplaced decimal point can cost a company a fortune.

This incident also shows that even if reporters think their story is going out to a "dead" audience—one that they can neither see nor hear—business journalists are listened to intently by those in the financial sector and beyond. Business journalists have a huge audience and a demanding one—which sets them apart from regular news reporters in the accuracy stakes.

The Big Three Newswire Agencies

One of the finest news agency journalists I ever worked with was a Dow Jones editor. Randy Walerius is an American who was at that time working for the Dow Jones/*Wall Street Journal* bureau in London. He is now back on US soil in Washington working with a specialist government unit for Bloomberg.

His view on the importance of newswires is that agencies such as Reuters, Bloomberg News, and Dow Jones are among the biggest news organizations in the world and have withstood the economic pressure of the past two decades better than many newspapers and magazines. The reason is simple. To varying degrees, the three companies provide information—news and data— to financial markets and charge a high price to do so.

The biggest financial newswire agencies sit within companies that sell a range of products. Dow Jones—part of News Corp—publishes *The Wall Street Journal* and other newspapers and magazines. Bloomberg owns *Bloomberg Business Week*. Reuters is part of Thomson Reuters, a company that owns special publications for lawyers and other professionals. All three companies cover not only business and financial markets but also politics, sports, culture, and more.

For the newswires within these companies, however, their bread and butter comes from selling information to the financial markets: stock, bond, com- modities, and currency markets. In fact, the growth of the agencies since the 1980s and their resilience today tracks the growth of financial markets around the globe. The financial sector is much bigger in the United States, Europe, and Japan than it used to be; and it is present in places like China, Russia, India, and Brazil where it used to be virtually nonexistent. Financial institutions are willing to pay lots of money for news that could change the value of trillions of dollars of assets.

The Role of the Newswire Agencies

To compete in that market and to justify the high subscriber fees, the agencies compete ruthlessly on speed, and their credibility depends on accuracy. Success is often measured by being fractions of a second faster than a competitor. If one customer in the financial markets gets the news slightly sooner than another, that customer—or more likely, that customer's computers—can buy or sell a financial instrument at a better price. The price advantage disappears, of course, as soon as the entire market responds to the same information.

Hundreds of millions or even billions of dollars' worth of trading can take place because of news that the US central bank is changing interest rates, for example, or that one company is making an offer to buy another company, or that Saudi Arabia will increase or decrease oil production, or that China's economic policy will raise the demand for copper. The news service that delivers that information to its customers first gives the customer a market advantage.

Rule of Thumb   The rule of thumb 20 years ago was that a trader who received information three seconds before others in the market had enough time to act on that news by buying or selling the relevant stocks, bonds, commodities, or currencies. Today, with most trading executed by fast computers, the time to act is down to milliseconds.

The major customers of the three biggest financial agencies—Dow Jones, Reuters, Bloomberg—are banks, hedge funds, companies, and other financial institutions. The news reaches them over computer terminals that also carry vast amounts of price and other financial data. The computers also have the functionality to manipulate that data into charts and other tools to help the traders think about prices. For the traders who use the terminals, the news typically takes up less of their screen space than the data. But the news is still essential for many of them.

Note   Powerful computers can digest ever greater amounts of information and find connections between seemingly unrelated items. That has increased the market's appetite for information in recent decades. Companies that once focused on domestic markets are now affected by actions on the other side of the world. Pension funds invest their money in assets—financial or physical—in many countries. A US economic slowdown will hurt Chinese exports. Droughts in Russia may drive up global wheat prices. European rules on carbon emissions may add a cost to US airlines.

So essential is this news that the companies that own these newswire agencies have some of the biggest editorial staffs in the world. Reuters and Bloomberg each have about 2,400 news professionals in offices around the world. Dow Jones, including *The Wall Street Journal*, has almost 2,000.

Reuters, Bloomberg, and Dow Jones station their employees in bureaus around the globe to gather and publish economic statistics from governments and central banks, earnings reports and other announcements from companies, weather conditions and crop yields, water levels on rivers and strikes at ports, car sales and airplane orders, and much more besides. They also cover elections, military conflicts, social unrest, and—because people who work in financial markets tend to like games—sports. The journalists seek out interviews with central bankers, finance ministers, chief executives, private equity fund managers, and others who can offer insight that's relevant to financial prices.

The United States, Europe, and Japan have the biggest economies and so are home to the biggest market centers and most of the world's biggest companies. The three agencies' biggest bureaus are therefore likely in New York, London, and Tokyo and other major cities. But Moscow, Beijing, and Dubai have become market centers in their own right. Reuters has staff in about 150 countries. Bloomberg has almost 150 bureaus in 72 countries.

The farther the agency bureau is from a modern financial market, the more effort the journalists may have to put in to obtain relevant news. Journalists in London and Berlin receive most of their information in electronic form, quickly digest it, and send it back out to their subscribers. Journalists in the Ivory Coast may travel through the cocoa belt to get a sense of how the crop looks; those in Vietnam may do the same to evaluate the coffee crop.

NEWS JUDGMENT

One way to think about news judgment in these agencies is to ask whether a piece of information may change the price of a stock, bond, commodity, or currency—or derivatives of those assets. If the answer is yes—or even just maybe—it's news. The reporter who obtains that information is paid to file it quickly and accurately. The headline encapsulates the actionable information and is often sufficient by itself for the purposes of financial market customers. The market relevance is obvious in the 60 or so characters of the headlines: "Bank of England Raises Interest Rates 25 Basis Points," "China Plans to Rein in Bank Lending," or "Toyota Raises Forecast for Car Sales in 2013."

Governments and Companies as Sources of News

The major sources of news are governments and companies. Government reports on economic activity such as inflation and retail sales and unemployment, as well as government policy announcements, provide a steady stream of information that the news agencies have to relay to their clients. Corporate reports on earnings, acquisitions and sales, and other activity provide a still faster flow of information because there are far more companies than there are governments in the world.

In advanced economies, governments release economic reports at regular intervals and under established rules, often in what is known as a "lockup." Journalists are literally locked in a room and allowed no contact with the outside world. They have about half an hour to digest the material in the government report. At a specified time, the communications lines are opened and the journalists send it out to the markets. In that half hour, the journalists have to be able to identify the main news, spot unexpected content in the economic data, formulate headlines that convey the main points, and write brief stories to back that up.

Think, for example, of a government report on inflation released monthly. The journalist in the lockup will identify main headlines that look something like these:

June Prices Rose 0.2 Percent from May, 1.7 Percent from June Last Year

or

Excluding Energy, June Inflation Was 0.1 Percent from May, 1.4 Percent from June Last Year

The journalists will also search through the government report to find other nuggets of information that may interest the markets. The pace at which food or housing prices are rising may be worthy for additional headlines.

By the time the communications lines are opened, the journalist will have formulated as many headlines as are necessary and the story to back those headlines up. In that story, the journalist will add context, possibly to explain why energy prices were a factor that month or why the market is interested in food or housing.

ACCURACY IS KEY

Because accuracy is so essential to this work, the agencies take special care to ensure it. They will typically have a policy that says no headline or story can be published without a second reader—a "second set of eyes" in agency jargon. And since speed is so important, that second reader may be standing behind the writer and reading the material over his or her shoulder. Those are minimum standards. Many stories are read by several editors; and the most sensitive stories—those that can damage reputations or investigative work that could have a broad impact on many markets—are likely to be read as often as a dozen times or more, including by the agency's own libel lawyers.

Modern companies—at least those listed on a modern stock exchange—will similarly release earnings under rules set by their regulators, although it is rarely as elaborate as a locked room. The companies send an earnings report, or a takeover announcement, or some other development to the main news agencies, which in turn relay the main points to the markets. As with government economic news, the journalists have to move extremely fast to identify what the market wants to know, formulate the necessary headlines and story, and publish.

In both the government economic news and the company reports, financial agency journalists play a crucial role in the modern financial regulatory structure. Insider trading—trading with information that should be available only to a few people—is illegal in many markets. By getting large amounts of information to large groups of traders at the same time, the agencies reduce the chance that any particular market participants will get information through illicit channels and use it to trade profitably.

As with most reputable news organizations, the financial news agencies are careful not to allow content to leak out to the market before it is published. That attitude is driven not only by the desire to ensure the integrity of the content; it's also driven by the realization that market participants could use even seemingly harmless information to profit. The agencies take this responsibility very seriously.

The Role of the Journalist within News Agencies

The agencies have teams of journalists with specific expertise. The economic experts know where to find the news quickly in a government report and the journalists assigned to cover companies know where to look in a company announcement for key information. Commodities journalists will have similar familiarity with supply and demand of things like oil, tin, wheat, or rice.

Fixed-income experts keep tabs on bond issuance and trends in interest rates. Foreign exchange coverage requires knowledge of economic forces that will cause traders to move from one currency to another.

In past decades, as the Internet has become prevalent, computers have become increasingly important in carrying out tasks that used to be done by journalists, or not at all. Computers can scan reports from governments or companies in seconds, finding the words that matter and even drawing conclusions from those words about whether they signal whether to buy or sell a specific financial instrument. If a central banker gives a speech in which he repeatedly—and perhaps unexpectedly—says he's "optimistic" about the economy, many financial market traders would know what to buy and sell without any quantitative help about the meaning of optimism.

■ **Example**   Several years ago, agencies and markets were watching the statements of the European Central Bank closely to see if the bank was "concerned" about inflation or "very concerned" about inflation. In this scenario, only one word more or less was needed to determine whether the bank had changed its thinking and the policy that would follow from that thinking.

As structured—or computerized—as the release of so much information is today, journalists at the financial news services have plenty of opportunity to take the initiative and find their own stories. Many events or developments are still unexpected. Oil wells explode, hurricanes shut down ports, disease strikes plants or animals or human beings, scientists make new discoveries that have commercial potential, and businesses spring up to challenge established companies. Not so long ago, companies such as Google and Facebook didn't exist. Today, they receive close attention from financial markets and from the financial news agencies that serve those markets.

Journalists have to be on the lookout for the things that aren't announced through official channels. They conduct interviews with government officials, company executives, fund managers, and others to gain news and insight that will be of interest to their market audience. They read reports, visit factories, watch consumer trends, and much more.

If, for example, a Russian energy company's financial reports show lack of investment in new equipment for many years, the journalist may draw the conclusion that the company will be able to produce less energy in the future. Energy markets around the world will be interested. Or if a European government official says in an interview that the European Union should consider a tax on financial transactions, the journalist will be able to tell the market about a potential additional cost of doing business that will fall on thousands of financial institutions and companies and individuals.

To manage the demands of so many areas of coverage that require so much expertise, the financial news agencies have to coordinate their own journalists to make sure the expertise is deployed effectively. That could require collaboration among energy journalists around the world or it could require collaboration among journalists in a single bureau whose tasks don't typically overlap.

Tip   For aspiring journalists, the financial news agencies are among the bright lights in the news business. Their broad coverage means the agencies need journalists with a much wider range of skills than most newspapers, and their global reach means the skilled journalists with the necessary language skills can find opportunities that aren't so easy to come by in other parts of the news business.

The Importance of Pictures

Most big news agencies now have a television arm. They feed news stories with pictures. One of the problems for these news agencies and especially some of the smaller wire services is to have video content that can be used to illustrate the stories in an attractive way.

Reuters had a huge library of film and video at one time, but even that huge agency was forced to recycle the same old footage of dollars or pounds rolling off the presses, the facades of the Bank of England, the Hong Kong Stock Exchange, or Wall Street, and the closing-bell ritual on the New York trading floor.

These pictures were known as "wall paper." The story was in the script and in the interviews or sound bites from financial experts. But as Jim Boulden, CNN's London correspondent, points out, television is a picture medium. A story depends as much, if not more, on its visual impact as on its script content.

The three big newswire agencies have hundreds of correspondents around the world. But even for them, gathering video material for every occasion and every event is a step too far. That limitation has given rise to picture agencies, which I cover in the next chapter.

Getting the Pictures

Images are an essential feature of journalism. They help tell the story.

Pictures—video or photographs—can bring the story to life, whereas words need supplements to reinforce details of the story. Whether it is the sedate opening of a parliament or a horrific story of a plane crash, images bring a story to life and are important to the telling of a tale.

General news requires photographs and video to illustrate a story and photojournalism has become an important arm of journalism. Photojournalists (and the term includes video) help interpret events and communicate newsworthy information through still or moving images, used in conjunction with a written story or sometimes on their own with nothing more than a caption. Some television news programs even run a sequence of video stories without commentary—usually captioned "No Comment"— relying on the moving pictures to tell the story on their own.

The News through Images

Photojournalists "write" with a camera and disseminate news events through images. Editors choose front-page pictures carefully to attract readers, but they also use photos to illustrate less important events through head-and-shoulders shots of the story's subject.

Editors argue that photographs in journalism inform, educate, and enlighten readers about current issues and enhance the credibility of stories, confirming the authenticity of a news story and providing proof that an event has actually occurred.

THINGS AREN'T ALWAYS WHAT THEY SEEM

As an editor, I used to subscribe to the Columbia Journalism Review, produced by students of the excellent journalism school at New York's Columbia University. A feature of the Review was showing a photograph that had appeared in a wide number of publications from around the world with different captions used for the same picture.

One example was the photo of a Boeing 737 jet standing on a runway. Captions varied from "Plane hijackers are holding hostages on board a New York bound plane" to "Boeing has unveiled its new short-haul aircraft."

Pictures for business news can vary wildly. Especially in television, dull pictures of banks, factories, and shopping malls are used extensively. But when the story is about the financial cost of natural events, such as hurricanes, forest fires, or devastating snowstorms, the images can be very dramatic and make a story come alive.

Radio is the poor cousin here, but almost all other media can use images to good effect. The important thing for any journalist is to treat the choice of pictures sensitively to ensure that false meaning isn't created and ethics aren't breached.

ETHICS IN PHOTOJOURNALISM

Ethics plays a great part in ensuring that this ideal—that photographs in journalism inform, educate, and enlighten—is met.

Editors can sometimes be cruel with photo manipulation. One UK newspaper, for example, published a photograph of Cherie Blair, wife of the former UK Prime Minister. The picture was of Mrs. Blair on a speaker's platform where two small flags had been situated. The photo made it look as if two horns were protruding from her head, giving her a satanic appearance. One columnist, on seeing this picture, dubbed the good lady "The Wicked Witch," and the name stuck.

Editors must also keep a strict eye on photos taken on mobile phones by citizen journalists. Those photos are not always what they purport to be.

Despite these cautions, photojournalism—both still photography and videography—can, used responsibly, make a news story very attractive to a reader and viewer. As long as it is honest, a picture can indeed be worth a thousand words.

The Challenge of Sourcing Pictures

Simon Brooksbank is the executive video editor for the European bureau of Getty Images, a giant US picture agency with an enviable reputation. But he entered the television news agency business at Reuters, working on a financial program called *Financial Report*. (*Financial Report* was shortened to FINREP, and so it was known within Reuters for a decade.)

This program was a review of the important business, economic, and financial news of the week and was transmitted to client television stations at 0300 on a Saturday morning. The timing was dictated by the closing time of the New York Stock Exchange, which was at 2100 GMT, so the program's final details had to be collated, scripted, and picture coordinated after that time before being sent via satellite to more than 80 TV stations worldwide.

The program was broadcast with a split track. A *split track* is a video report that is produced with an English-language commentary but is formatted so that a client newsroom can ignore the English voice-over and have its own newsreader provide a commentary, reading from the script provided. Brooksbank was assistant producer on the show and part of his job was to make sure suitable video was available to "cover" the script. This need not be too complicated for a 2'40" news package, but for a half-hour program it was a nightmare.

The scripting of the program began on Thursdays. The news of the week was collated and the events likely to occur on Thursday and Friday were noted from one of the big news agency diary companies. Brooksbank helped research the stories, discussed the importance of each with me, and helped produce a running order.

▰ **Note**   My role was as producer. In other words, if there were any errors in the program, it was my head on the block with fierce line editors in offices tucked well away from the newsroom floor relishing the opportunity to cut it off if any errors were made.

But Brooksbank also had the tough job of sourcing picture content from video stock content, which was then held in Reuters' own library. All news video from correspondents, camera crews, client television stations, and independent producers was recorded, logged, and put into a huge library. For FINREP, Brooksbank would digest the stories, look at catalogued video and the week's news coverage, and begin to compile the available footage that was suitable to "paint" onto the script.

He also had access to the then-many PR and VNR (video news release) companies that distributed video stock content for free around the media in a bid to get coverage for their clients. This VNR material was a godsend because the producers of it were anxious to see the use of pictures of their clients' products, which could range from cars to airplanes. It was a terrific source of content, as it was well shot, edited, and presented and could vary from auto manufacturing to hi-tech engineering to bank notes being printed to coffee beans being picked.

As FINREP was a voice-led program, it was a case of painting images over the script to best illustrate what was being reported. The trick was to keep looking for more of the same, as monotonous repetition had to be avoided to keep the show fresh. Brooksbank needed to supply us with many different shots of, say, coffee beans being picked, so it didn't feel as though we were rehashing the same shots. As and when he found good clips, he'd compile them on to master tapes (Beta SP back then), and he'd just keep building the archive.

All this material was collected over the two days, with the activity for getting suitable pictures getting more frenzied as the hours ticked by on a Friday.

If, for example, a hurricane started wreaking destruction somewhere in the world around about supper time, then Brooksbank had to go chasing the pictures, trying to determine if they would come in by satellite in time to be used over the inevitable coffee prices story or the Lloyds' insurance story related to the damage the storms had created.

But that was then. This background led Brooksbank to his job as executive producer at Getty Images, one of today's leading providers of stock images and video.

Presentation Is Key

Today, the content of business reporting hasn't changed that much, but Brooksbank is in accord with Jim Boulden that viewers' expectations are higher when it comes to production values. Content is easier to acquire now that we live in a global village, and so there's no excuse for poor quality of presentation and video.

Brooksbank says, "This makes the hunt for the best quality content exciting—the thrill of the chase as it were … and when we find a unique filmmaker in some far flung region who has unique content that's rarely been seen who wants to partner up, that's a good day."

▨ **Note** There has been a long-held belief among many news producers that American television understands news presentation rather better than their UK counterparts but that the Brits pay more attention to the news content. I've often been in hot debates about the veracity of this view, and my personal opinion is that the two news cultures have come closer together in recent years.

THE ABILITY TO SHOP AROUND FOR NEWS

News content, no matter how good, won't on its own attract a viewer, and most certainly won't keep a viewer's attention. But audiences are often more sophisticated than the profession gives them credit for and presentation alone won't cover up sloppy journalism, bad reporting, and a naïve selection of stories. Now that access to hundreds of TV channels is available, the viewer and you can "shop and compare." News channels, whether dedicated totally to business such as CNBC or general news with business content as in BBC World News, are commonplace on TV screens. Watch carefully, make a comparison, and both assess whether the content versus presentation debate is still valid and see which news channel becomes your favorite after taking a view on the debate.

Today, Brooksbank's job is to ensure the broadcaster has the widest possible choice of moving pictures or "images." He has a counterpart at Getty who deals in still photography, and this setup is pretty much the same in all the other big picture agencies: Reuters, Associated Press Television News (APTN), and Agence France-Presse. There are hundreds of other smaller news agencies and some that are based on national demands, such as Russia's RIA Novosti and China's Xinhua.

How Getty Images and Other Picture Agencies Work

How do these agencies gather their news pictures from around the world?

First, Getty Images, for instance, has 90 million still images and 1.3 million video clips available on its website and is available in more than 100 countries. This volume obviously grows as new pictures and video are submitted. The stills and video run across news, sport, entertainment, and creative stock. Photos and stills are more suitable to features rather than news.

News organizations (as well as advertising agencies, moviemakers, documentary producers, and others) can search the site under different categories for the images they want and buy them online, ready to use in a news bulletin or documentary.

Modern technology has made this capability available on demand. But when I first worked at Reuters, correspondents were still shooting a story on video (very occasionally on film, depending on which country the story was happening in), driving to the airport, handing the video to the pilot of a friendly airline on the end of a long pole, and thus "air mailing" it to London, Paris, New York, or some other major news center. A dispatch rider would then be waiting at the airport of choice to whisk the tape to the newsroom where it would be edited and put on a daily satellite feed to various countries.

Reuters, for instance, sent a daily feed containing half a dozen or more stories via satellite to Latin America—the video all carefully edited and scripted for use. But the delays were obvious. What happened today might not arrive at distant television stations until the day after tomorrow, so news in pictures was always broadcast well after the fact. For business news, this was disastrous because, as you will have gathered from other items in this book, business news needs to be almost instantaneous so that financial markets can decide where the money should go.

■ **Note** Instant availability has become an attractive option for news and business news organizations, especially as the "breaking news" concept has taken hold among nearly all global news broadcasters.

Today Getty is representative of other stock agencies with around 35 million searches for content each month. So the agency has teams of creative researchers who compile lists of the sort of content people have been searching for but can't find. This is translated by the editorial department into searching for, developing, and displaying different versions of images already on the site but with a different angle. This enables Getty editors to be very specific when it comes to collecting data of what is needed to better fulfill the demands of the market and to plug content gaps. The data is collected and collated by the researchers who then let editorial know where, when, or if the content emphasis should be changed.

The trends make interesting reading, especially for editors and publishers who need to know what their readership or viewership is and how it is changing. In 2013, for example, the key areas of focus were Brazil, Japan, and the German language regions, where demand for content has grown enormously.

The trend information might be general—for example, which region is demanding what sort of images. But editors then know exactly what is needed and from where. This enables them to target very specific producers who may have shot films or documentaries in these countries and then persuade them to change their spots and swap the role of client into supplier, offering in exchange some of the material they have shot for sale on the Getty site.

WHAT TO DO WITH EXTRA MATERIAL

Often, producers and directors of documentaries never think that the extra material they have shot (and some companies will shoot a ratio of 15:1—that is, for every minute of video used, they shoot for 15 minutes) is useful. For example, images of monkeys swinging in trees could be very useful for a news item that is about decimation of the rainforests. Clients often have specific types of content they never thought would be of any value beyond the production for which they were originally intended.

Keeping Imagery Current

As noted in Chapter 11, "wall papering" a business story is no longer acceptable. Business news is now headline news as often as not, and both print and video enterprises need to make their stories attractive. The standard shots of Wall Street and the Bank of England are no longer acceptable.

So the big picture agencies keep a "needs" list that applies to all countries globally, and they always need updated versions of all business-related images on every topic. For example, it is no longer acceptable to run pictures of trading floors with dealers dressed in multicolored jackets and waving their arms. The electronic age has taken over, and while the pictures of these animated traders made for exciting television, the truth now is that dealers sit transfixed by a computer screen. Not as exciting, but the video still needs to be up to date.

Business news also requires quite straightforward shots, pretty much everything from industry, manufacturing, agriculture, shipping, mining, retail, banking, renewable energy, and so on—or, as Brooksbank puts it, "Basically every aspect of the beating heart of any and every country."

But these images are finite. A picture of a factory belching out smoke is useless if the country it is in has passed stiff clean air laws, and an old picture of a building on a green field site is inappropriate if the business has expanded or other buildings have grown up around it. Business news is no different than other news. Images must be fresh and up to date.

The Business of Video Clips

Picture agencies generally have video teams in London, New York, and Los Angeles, and video content is also acquired from allied contributors. Getty, along with other major news agencies, makes great efforts to find suitable contributors and then mentor them so they supply suitable content that is technically competent.

In the very competitive television world, the video content of business programs has become increasingly important. So Getty, Reuters, and others have correspondingly taken on key roles.

But, much as this resource is valued, it is still up to producers and editors to make sure their choice of pictures is as suitable to the content as they can make it. Gone are the days where the same pictures of The Bank of England or Federal Reserve can be simply pasted onto a voice. The audience is now much more sophisticated and won't tolerate such a slovenly way of presentation. And no production team—least one that has put together a business news item—wants to lose an audience.

New Media

Neither do men put new wine into old bottles: else the bottles break, and the wine runneth out, and the bottles perish: but they put new wine into new bottles, and both are preserved.

—Matt. 9:17

But can you put old media into new technologies without the old media perishing?

Opinion is divided on this question. Many advocates of new media claim that the advent of modern communications systems is whittling away at traditional forms of media and will eventually cause the demise of print and electronic media as we now know it. Traditionalists point to the fact that the newspaper industry has taken a hit but is now holding up well, while terrestrial/satellite TV stations continue to proliferate.

Both sides have passionate advocates of the value and sustainability of one type of media or the other, which has led to entrenched positions.

The Past, Present, and Future of the Media

In the 1950s, with the advent of television, radio was supposed to disappear. It fought back with the introduction of disc jockeys and phone-in hosts. TV forced radio to change and in some ways improve. TV also eroded the movie industry, until Hollywood hit back with blockbusters and multiscreen cinemas.

The changes in the industry have historically come from conflict between different media, which have certainly not expired but persist in a somewhat different form today. The Web has forced TV, newspapers, and magazines to change, but the prophets of doom and gloom for traditional media should temper their forecasts that newspapers and TV have a terminal illness.

Anyone who claims social media will eliminate mass media is failing to look at the statistics. In the United States, for example, there has been an overall decline in viewing figures on the old-fashioned boob tube. But according to Nielsen, television viewing numbers on all devices are beginning to rise again.

■ **Note** What is changing is technology, which is indifferent to program content. Surveys show more people in both America and Britain using computers, tablets, and smartphones to watch TV, but they still watch traditional programming.

Newspapers have lost circulation in most Western countries over a decade, but they have increased in developing nations, especially Africa. Nonetheless, there are still more than 160 million people annually buying newspapers in the United States (according to the Newspaper Association of America) and more than 30 million in the UK (according to the Audit Bureau of Circulation).

New technology has certainly reduced the number of people a newspaper or TV station employs, and there is certainly a shift in audiences for all traditional media. But I suspect that the quote attributed to Mark Twain over his own obituary—"The report of my death was an exaggeration"—may well apply to traditional media.

My guess is that there will be sharp changes in the way traditional media operates but less of a dramatic impact from new media. The chances are that they will use each other as they develop, bringing the strengths of each genre to a general development of future news media.

One thing is for sure. The development and continuing changes in open markets throughout the world have given a huge new pool of stories for the business journalist to trawl and that is to be savored for now.

The Future of the News Industry

Stephen Claypole is a former colleague and friend who, after a distinguished career at BBC News and Executive Editor at Reuters, set up the TV news arm of Associated Press, APTV, now called APTN. Claypole is now chairman of a thriving independent television production company, and I regularly meet him in that capacity for a glass of wine and to discuss the state of the TV sector generally and chat over any bright ideas we might have in helping to develop new television news enterprises.

But at each of these meetings, he cautions about getting carried away with electronic and new media as a panacea for the survival of broadcasting.

"We are," Claypole says, "or should be content providers. That is the important element of the news business." By this he means that news people should gather and assemble news and information rather than fret about the distribution medium.

I believe that in many ways he is right, although I can also have deep discussions with other senior journalists who take the opposite view and believe new media is the answer to almost everything and has a very different future than the one that the news industry faces right now.

New Media Journalism and the Citizen Journalist

The creation of the Internet has resulted in blogs, news sites, web sites, podcasts, and video opportunities such as YouTube. Today professional journalists and individuals alike can offer news to the masses. This change in content provider and delivery method has become known as "new media journalism."

The obvious advantage to professional journalists has been the speed with which news can be delivered, including live coverage via mobile phone. But the headache is that so-called citizen journalists—ordinary individuals who see, hear, or identify something—eagerly submit voice, text, and video from a phone while actually witnessing some unusual activity.

So far, so good. But then an intake editor or desk journalist has to take the decision about the authenticity of the events a nonprofessional is reporting. Even video pictures can be open to interpretation and can be seen from a viewpoint that doesn't necessarily reflect the facts.

That doesn't mean to say that citizen journalists aren't a valuable addition to the way news is collected. But it does mean that professional journalists need to be extra vigilant before passing on to the public the information sent to them for all the reasons that are outlined in the chapter on ethics.

But new media journalism isn't confined to the activities of citizen journalists. Anyone can now write a blog, set up their own web site, or run their own radio and TV station on the Web. And many will applaud the fact that this sort of journalism is now available to the average person. After all, don't we all have opinions of one sort or another and shouldn't we be free to express them?

Policing the New Media

But who monitors these new outlets? Who is there to be "editor" of the information, to ensure that expressions of opinion are not libelous or causing harm to innocent individuals?

The recent phone hacking scandal by journalists and senior editors at the now defunct *News of the World* newspaper has demonstrated that established media has been found wanting in controlling its news-gathering activities and has been used by some advocates of new media as good reason to give citizen journalism free rein.

The other argument is that the law can protect people from libel and false reporting. Indeed, so it can, but sometimes not until an individual or enterprise has had its reputation blackened beyond repair.

A recent UK court case found that messages on Twitter posted by Sally Bercow, the wife of the Speaker of the British House of Commons, were defamatory. Bercow sent a text on the social media service implying that a member of the aristocracy, Lord McAlpine, was linked to a child sex abuse case. Others made the same claim and were eventually brought before the courts. Bercow denied malicious intent, but the court ruled that the damage had been done: McAlpine was in the public eye a pedophile.

McAlpine's solicitor, Andrew Reid of RMPI LLP, said, with some justification, that the court judgment against Bercow "provides both a warning to, and guidance for, people who use social media. It highlights how established legal principles apply to social media, and how the courts take account of the particular way in which social media operates when reaching decisions on whether publications are defamatory."[1]

For having recycled the libel, the BBC and ITV, Britain's leading broadcasters, reached out-of-court settlements with McAlpine, who also successfully pursued judgments against individual re-tweeters. The case highlights the danger to established media of rushing to report from new media without adequate vetting.

The McAlpine case occurred in a sophisticated civil society. There are still many countries, however, where the only qualification to be a journalist is simply to say, "I am a journalist." So the dangers of misreporting and unprofessional conduct are often very close to the surface when new media is used to pass on news.

---

[1] Peter Dominiczak, "Court Rules against Sally Bercow over her 'Innocent Face' McAlpine Tweet," *The Telegraph*, May 24, 2013. http://www.telegraph.co.uk/news/uknews/crime/10078119/Court-rules-against-Sally-Bercow-over-her-innocent-face-McAlpine-tweet.html

A Change in Traditional News Organizations

Technology and new media have had a profound impact on the way that traditional news organizations operate. The sector has become congested with news, fragmenting sources and altering target audiences for all types of media. The number of web sites specializing in new media journalism has grown so large and popular that there are now major players in the field, such as the US's conservative *Drudge Report* (www.drudgereport.com) and liberal *The Huffington Post* (www.huffingtonpost.com).

Traditional media profess a neutral stance (disingenuously, many critics argue), but many new media outlets abandon all pretence at neutrality and expound opinion on their web sites, leaving the readers to make up their own minds about the veracity of the information published. But many journalists from established media have set up their own independent blogs, bringing a new professionalism to the new media sector; while, conversely, many traditional outlets have introduced new media journalism platforms to multiply their outlets to the public.

The style of traditional journalism has changed to accommodate the use of new media by adding online editions to the still flourishing newspaper sector. New journalism is no longer constrained by space or time, in contrast to the constraints binding traditional newspaper editors, who have to calculate how many stories they want in a given edition and how many words to allow reporters to fill in the spaces allotted for each story.

As a very young reporter, I worked for a very experienced Canadian editor on a Vancouver weekly, *The Lions Gate Times*. He sent me to cover the premiere of a film version of James Joyce's *Ulysses*.

It's a complicated plot, but I wrote a magnificent article (by my own reckoning) and proudly submitted the copy. When I read the article in the newspaper, it finished halfway through the story I had written and in mid-sentence. The editor had been ruthless. I had exceeded my words, and he had no space in the paper to let me get away with it.

Radio and TV are even more unforgiving. A five-minute news bulletin is a five-minute news bulletin: no more, no less. Time is precious in mainstream electronic media. And in a long career in electronic media, I was only once ever allowed to go over time, and that was under exceptional circumstances.

I was hosting a radio program on the problems of alcoholism. To demonstrate how the effects can creep up on you without you realizing it, the engineers set up a series of skills tests in the studio, such as a device that set off a bell. I had to react to the bell by hitting a button. Throughout the program I drank beer at the rate I would at a social function, and as I attempted to perform each task, my reaction time was posted. At the end of the program, I was certainly not drunk, but my reaction time had been considerably extended. But the cardinal sin was that I ran two minutes over program time. I was never allowed to do that ever again either on radio or TV.

So space and time are restricting factors for text and electronic media. But one of the advantages of new media is that a story can be as long as a writer wants it to be. The shackles are off.

A COMMENT ON THE HABITS OF TODAY'S READERS

Whether a reader wants long pieces of text is another matter. Already critics complain that politicians of every color and every nation no longer read at all. But whether that is general among the populace is debatable.

I would only point to the fact that Britain's best-selling daily paper, *The Sun*, is dominated by pictures, includes very catchy headlines, and has limited text—there is almost no in-depth reporting. Perhaps that says something about the reading habits of much of the general population.

The Literature of the Everyday

When it comes to a writing style for new media, the adage—"The golden rule is that there is no golden rule"—really comes into its own. Because there are really no rules governing writing for new media.

The guidelines outlined earlier in this book about writing styles for newspapers and TV ought in principle to apply as much to new media as to traditional news outlets, perhaps allowing for a little more license than traditional media does for a free-flowing style. But those who practiced new media in its infancy were mostly from the world of literature and set out to cast off the constraints, as they saw them, of the newswriting style of late 20th- and early 21st-century newspapers.

It is a bit more difficult to modify the style of writing for radio and television, because the ear and the eye react reflexively to the terse, cryptic writing required by electronic media. But many TV journalists now have to write for a TV station's web version and so must master both styles.

The style for new media—if there is one—has been described as the "literature of the everyday." And so it is. No one blog will be quite like any other. Twitter has its own language. And personal web sites reflect the idiosyncratic style of the individual writer.

Each of us has our own way of expressing ourselves in written language, from grammar and word usage to retailing slang and the language of the street. The famous legless World War II fighter pilot Douglas Bader is quoted as saying, "Rules are for the obedience of fools and the guidance of wise men." That seems to be good advice for how to write for new media: let yourself go, but don't write so that no one has any idea what you are writing about.

Blog authors tend to write in such a way that their ideas flow freely: a stream-of-consciousness style of writing. Others retain a formality, their style born of the discipline of newswriting of the last century and the strict style format under which they served their apprenticeships.

Note   I must confess that I have been penning text for newspapers and television so long that breaking away from a more formal style proves exceedingly difficult. But with new media, it doesn't matter. I can more or less write in any way that takes my mood.

But don't fall into the trap of ignoring the basic news principles outlined in various parts of this book. If you are reporting on important events, then make sure both guidelines and style are dictated by the audience and the gravity of the subject.

Write all you want in any style you want; but if no one bothers to read it, your sense of satisfaction at what you wrote can drain away very rapidly. As a journalist, you still have an irreducible responsibility for your output and must always strive for credibility.

Out with the Old?

New media writing can be very satisfying. It is writing that comes from deep within you. It is yours.

I am an old skeptic. I always believed that good journalists had an overdose of skepticism in their veins. It helped them to get to the truth of a story, to write as the facts dictate and the audience demands.

I have my doubts whether the freedom of new media will eventually overtake or even destroy traditional media, as some believe. But if that day should come, I must either adapt to the new media or die with the old.

Only time will tell what the outcome will be.

Key Points

- Today's news people should be "content providers"—that is, they should gather and assemble news and information—rather than worry about the distribution medium.

- The Internet has brought us new media journalism, enabling professional journalists and individuals alike to write news for the masses. But with this new freedom comes new responsibilities.

- Although basic journalistic principles apply when writing for new media, the formats associated with new media allow for the expression of more personal, free-form views.

Macroeconomics

Each individual nation has an economy of its own, which is more about general statistics than the type of business data found in a specific type of market. This is known as *macroeconomics*.

Macroeconomic data is basically examining facts and figures to reflect how healthy an economy is. And there are some statistics related to macroeconomics that are vital to understanding what is happening to a country and any impact those events might have globally.

The US non-farm payroll data, for example, is important to the United States but is also eagerly watched by market analysts the world over. American unemployment can and does have an impact on the global economy and must be watched by business journalists wherever they are.

Economists use a range of information to gauge economic health such as employment figures (non-farm payroll in the United States), *gross domestic product* (GDP) money supply, consumer prices, producer prices, and retail sales data.

This information can indicate whether there is a recession or prosperity looming; what government can do about it; which part of society will be affected; how much items in, say, a supermarket cost; and if there are any inflationary fears to look out for.

In other words, macroeconomics tells us how a country is doing financially.

So this is an area that business journalists need to understand and keep an eye on. They need to be able to tell people what they can expect in cost of living, employment, rising prices, and other events that will affect how we all live and support ourselves.

A MEASURE OF THE US AND WORLD ECONOMIES

Each month, the US Department of Labor Statistics releases a report about the number of people employed in manufacturing and construction as one of the indicators of the growth or shrinkage of the US economy. As its title, non-farm payroll data, implies, it does not include workers in agriculture or the nonprofit sector.

This employment report is considered very carefully in global financial markets because it will dictate the value of the dollar, foreign exchange markets, and bond and stock markets.

The numbers are compared month by month, and when they are buoyant a collective sigh of relief is heard around the financial world. Job losses bring dark clouds of gloom over the financial sector and the state of the global economy suffers.

Key Economic Measures

From the indicators just mentioned, economists take as key measures of economic prosperity national income, unemployment figures, inflation, and international trade data.

National Income and Gross Domestic Product

National income is the measure of the **monetary value of the flow of output of goods and services** produced in an economy over a 12-month period and is a measure of economic growth, changes to living standards, and the distribution of income.

A NEED FOR ACCURATE MODELS

Because a national economy is extremely complex, economists have followed the KISS (keep it simple, stupid) advice given to journalists; they have tried to simplify the data contained in economic reports so that others can readily identify the main points of interest or concern. This is because they need to both understand very quickly the economic state of a nation but also apply the statistics to "models" that attempt to predict what the trends are and how to prepare for future problems—that is, how the system as a whole may be expected to behave. Economists strive to produce as accurate models as possible so that governments can develop successful development plans and policies for the national economy, thus promoting growth and overall prosperity.

The more widely used indicator of a country's economic health is GDP, which is the total value of output in an individual economy that measures the change in economic activity.

GDP includes capital investment, government spending, exports of goods and services, imports, and the output of foreign owned businesses that are located in a country (as long as they are the result of direct foreign investment). GDP is also calculated on the incomes from workers, private enterprise profits, and rents in the private sector.

GDP is usually measured in a common currency, and the **US dollar** is widely used. Exchange rates are notoriously volatile, so to provide more accuracy to the worldwide measurement of GDP, economists put a "basket" of goods and services common to most countries and look at the prices of the contents of that basket in different countries.

For example, the UK basket is made up of items that the average household purchases regularly and includes such things as breakfast cereals, chocolates, fruit, beer, computers, and even baby wipes. The basket is reviewed each year to make sure it reflects the purchasing habits of the average family. A sample of goods in the American basket can include new vehicles, airline fares, and gasoline.

Most of these indicators in the United States are released by various government departments. Non-farm payroll numbers are released monthly, the Bureau of Economic Accounts gives out GDP data, and the *consumer price index* (CPI) is measured by the Bureau of Labor Statistics (monthly), as is the *producer price index* (PPI). Retail sales come weekly from the US Census Bureau, and money supply statistics come from the Federal Reserve Board.

Note Money supply data is quite complicated and new journalists should research the various grades of the meaning of money supply from M0, which contains bank reserves in the calculations, to M3, which includes large deposits. M2 is the main indicator and is used in the measurement of inflation.

The agencies in other countries vary, but governments use broadly the same indicators to assess the strength of their national economies. For example, in the UK, monthly unemployment figures come from the Office of National Statistics, as does CPI, PPI, and retail sales. Money supply data is provided by The Bank of England.

All this data is available on the web sites of the responsible organizations.

Most journalists working in the big newswire agencies such as Reuters will have direct contacts in the agencies and banks, so for the average business journalist, using the wire services is probably the wisest way to go.

The wire services "flash" important figures, generally with some description of what they will mean to either the national or global economies. The commentary is written by real experts.

THE EFFECT OF TRANSFERS ON GDP

A word of caution about the commonly used term "transfers"; this usually means the private transfer of money from one individual to another. Such transactions are not usually taken into account in developed economies when GDP is calculated.

During the various wars across Europe in the last two decades of the 20th century, many people fled from the countries in conflict to more stable countries nearby. For example, many citizens of the Western Balkans fled to Germany, France, and the UK.

They flourished in these countries and now send substantial funds back to relatives, who remained in economies that are still very weak by international standards. These funds are known as "transfers," and the state of the national economy or GDP would be very different if these transfers were not taken into account.

Unemployment

Unemployment or joblessness is measured as those people who are out of work but want to work and are looking for jobs. It does not include people who are permanently on social benefits, including sick or disabled people who cannot work.

High levels of unemployment are costly to any economy, established or emerging. Such costs include unemployment benefit costs, other benefit payments, and lower tax revenues because unemployed individuals not only receive benefits but also pay no income tax. And because most unemployed people spend less, they contribute less to the government in indirect taxes, such as sales tax.

Unemployment also causes a waste of scarce economic resources and reduces the long-run growth potential of the economy—the man-hours that the unemployed do not work are lost forever.

As Europe has discovered, high and persistent unemployment can also have high security costs. The Eurozone economic crisis of the last decade has created wealth inequality across formerly stable EU member states such as Spain, Italy, Greece, and Portugal. Other EU members have had to make huge contributions to try and save the economies of these nations with only limited success. As a consequence, citizens have taken to the streets in violent and volatile demonstrations against their own governments, membership in the European Union, subscribing to the Euro currency, and the widespread lack of jobs.

This is costly to governments but also threatens the breakup of an economic union that seeks to expand, not lose members, and the loss of confidence of its unemployed citizens. Such protests are not confined to the EU but have taken place in many other countries around the globe as the worldwide economic crisis struck.

All these factors have a negative effect on long-term economic growth. Unemployment can harm growth not only because it is a waste of resources but also because it drives people to poverty, constrains liquidity (limiting labor mobility), and erodes self-esteem (promoting social dislocation, unrest, and conflict).

Inflation

Economists worry about inflation all the time and so do financial journalists. It is something that is key to a healthy economy and bears watching.

Inflation occurs when an economy suffers a persistent increase in the general price level of goods and services over a period of time. When price levels rise, for example, the pound or dollar buys fewer goods and services, resulting in a reduction in the purchasing power per pound or dollar.

Inflation is generally seen as bad for an economy; it means an increase in the cost of holding money, discourages investment and savings, triggers price rises, and then impacts on employers as workers demand higher wages to compensate for loss of currency value. In other words, their paycheck buys less.

The task of keeping the rate of inflation low and stable is usually given to a nation's central bank (The Bank of England in the UK or the Federal Reserve in the United States are examples), which sets interest rates. The theory is that higher interest rates curb spending, thereby relieving pressure on levels of inflation. High interest rates and slow growth of the money supply are the traditional ways through which central banks fight or prevent inflation.

The inflation rate is usually measured through the CPI, which measures movements in prices of a fixed basket of goods and services purchased by a "typical consumer." In the UK, the *retail prices index* (RPI) is added as a measure of inflation and contains a larger basket of goods and services.

Note Don't confuse monetary policy with a government's fiscal policy. Fiscal policy is how the government uses its taxes and budgets its cash. As a journalist you should watch for changes in the level and composition of taxation, government spending, and levels of borrowing.

International Trade Data

International trade is the exchange of goods, services, and capital across national borders. Countries such as the United States and political units such as the European Union believe in free trade—in other words the less restriction put on trading between countries, the better.

However, countries will periodically impose tariffs, which form a barrier to free trade. Tariffs are usually imposed to protect industries or sectors of a country against imported goods that undercut the price of a domestic product; they are taxes on imports that make imported goods more expensive and less competitive.

The European Union, for example, is fiercely protective of its agricultural sector and has imposed a tariff (import tax) of up to 75% on some meat and dairy products to discourage foreign imports. The United States protected its tire industry by slapping a 35% tax on imports from China.

Apart from tariffs, some countries impose quotas on imports and sometimes embargoes, a total ban on the imports of certain goods.

In 1994, the World Trade Organization (WTO) was established and is the only global international organization dealing with the rules of trade between nations. Almost all the world's trading nations, large and small, subscribe to the WTO, which grew from earlier negotiations under an international body known as the General Agreement on Tariffs and Trade (GATT).)

Belonging to the WTO means a country has signed a legal document that provides the ground rules for international commerce and to help trade flow as freely as possible between nations.

Associated with international trade are a country's balance of payments, which are the payments made for imports and exports. Balance of payments, like a commercial balance sheet, must always balance. Any trade deficit must be balanced with foreign investment, a decline in national reserves, or increased debt; likewise a trade surplus will be balanced out with financial outflows or increased reserves.

The Central Banks

Referring back to central banks, The Bank of England, affectionately known as "The Old Lady of Threadneedle Street" because it has existed on the same site since 1734, and the US Federal Reserve, formed in 1912 and also with affection called The Fed, are probably the best known central banks. But all countries have one, some quite new, and others having a life that stretches back in time.

A central bank is an institution that manages a state's monetary policy, which includes currency, money supply, and interest rates. In some countries they have responsibility for the commercial banking system. The central banks can increase the money supply, in some countries even printing the banknotes of the nation's currency. Usually the Bank sets a policy that promotes economic growth and stability.

In most of the developed economies, the central bank is independent from the government and is run by a type of chief executive usually known as a governor.

The big central banks are very cautious and usually signal to the financial community if they are about to make a significant change, even a small percentage point, in interest rates.

Economic analysts at major commercial banks and brokerages keep a very careful eye on interest rates and generally there is a consensus among them before an announcement is made about whether rates will rise, fall, or stay static and by what percentage. Mostly they are correct, and journalists will have a fair idea about the probability of an interest rate change.

The Bank of England's Monetary Policy Committee, which meets monthly, announces its decision following its meeting, always on a Thursday and always at noon. The Bank has a diary of meeting dates on its web pages. It alerts financial newswire services and simultaneously puts the decision on its own web pages.

In Washington, The Federal Reserve's Open Market Committee meets eight times a year but can increase that if any crises threaten the national economy and the Committee needs to take immediate action.

When central banks raise their prime rate, commercial banks do likewise and this in turn affects mortgage rates, car loans, business loans, and other consumer loans; so the business journalist has a plethora of stories to file once an interest rate change is announced.

Reporting on Macroeconomics

Macroeconomics is usually reported by specialist journalists in the field who deal with government officials, bankers, trade organizations, and the bond market experts. As with most market sectors, there are analysts who follow each of the macroeconomic elements of the economy, and it is wise to get to know a few who can be helpful.

Often, especially in broadcast news, macroeconomics and microeconomics are treated as two separate worlds. PBS's *Morning* and *Nightly Business* Reports were almost entirely focused on micro, while Reuters Financial Report was almost exclusively macro.

Of course there has to be a mix, but understanding the difference and focusing on one area of economic reporting is probably the way to being a specialist reporter to whom all others turn.

Key Points

- The US non-farm payroll data is a key global economic indicator.

- **The gross domestic product (GDP)**—the total value of output in an individual economy—is the measure of change in economic activity.

- Unemployment data is an important statistic, as unemployment can cause a series of problems for government.

- Inflation occurs when an economy suffers a persistent increase in the general price level of goods and services over a period of time.

- The task of keeping the rate of inflation low and stable is usually given to a nation's central bank.

- International trade is governed by the World Trade Organization (WTO).

- Journalists who report on macroeconomics are usually specialists in this field and have key contacts within the government and key financial institutions.

Globalization and the Interdependence of Small Economies

Facts rarely, if ever, stand alone. Journalists must add the context that gives the facts meaning. Even the biggest events are rarely so big that journalists don't have to start explaining immediately to their audience what their significance is. When countries elect new leaders, when countries go to war, or when major policies are adopted, journalists have to report the fact along with the explanation—that is, the global or local impact of such an event. Where business and economic news is concerned, this context often has to do with activity in neighboring economies. Reporting on these economies is the focus of this chapter.

Local Events Lead to Global Changes

Globalization can be as simple as a hurricane devastating a section of the coastline in the United States, but causing consumer goods prices in the United Kingdom to rise because of the storm's affect on crops, buildings, transport, and other consequences of a natural disaster.

Of course there are more sophisticated examples, such as the world watching the outcome of an American presidential election, aware that the candidates have made a number of election promises connected to US trade or economic policy. Depending on who wins, governments worldwide will need to review their trade dealings with the United States and adapt if necessary.

So events in one country will have an impact on another and nowhere more so than in the new economies of the Third World.

■ **Note** Because of modern communications, many such events will have an instant impact. Therefore, reporters need to be aware of what could happen as well as be able to react quickly to what does happen.

Business in Emerging Democracies

At one time, interaction was usually important only for business dealings in the major economies. But the collapse of the Soviet Empire, the emergence of dozens of new democracies, and a steady shift in the economic power of nations big and small has made global business reporting important to the world economic scene. A trade dispute in Belarus with Russia, for example, can affect the price of oil in France, which along with many other European countries is served by a pipeline that crosses Belarus from Russia.

Because Western governments have placed a good deal of political capital and huge amounts of funding into developing new democracies into open market economies, journalists need to be aware of any report on events in these countries, both as they affect each other but also as they affect the Western powers. So awareness of cross-border issues in the old Eastern Europe, the Balkans, and the Baltics, for example, is now a prime consideration for business reporters in London and New York.

Slowly local newswire services are beginning to start up in some of the emerging democracies. But reporters there, as I have pointed out in other parts of the book, are not very experienced. This is not to belittle them; but it is not much more than 15 years ago that they were working in centrally planned economies, business was a dirty word, and commercial competition was frowned on. It is not surprising then that they lack experience in reporting on business and economic affairs.

Nonetheless, their economies grow in importance year by year, and Western journalists need information from on the ground to be able to gauge what impact any of these given countries have on the global stage.

Many of these countries tend to be copycats. If one small country starts a privatization program, the bordering state will start to do likewise. Inexperienced reporters often don't see that a policy change has taken place and are left behind in reporting as important business stories begin to shape up.

There has been some effort by agencies such as the US Agency for International Development (USAID), the UN, Britain's Foreign Office, and other Western countries to try to remedy the situation by funding training courses. But aid funds are limited, local media is still financially poor, and new local governments are still deeply suspicious of allowing media access to information.

A new breed of business journalist is needed in these countries, and perhaps Western media should be more proactive in trying to help develop business reporting skills there.

Whatever the solution, Western media needs business news from these regions as they mature into full open market economies.

Domestic News in a Global Economy

Globalization has made it impossible to see economic and business events just as domestic news. Workers cross borders, products are exported and imported, and companies seek markets elsewhere when they have done as much as they can in their domestic market. With capital mostly free to flow effortlessly around the world, one country's interest rates or fiscal policy will have at least some effect if not great effect on investment decisions in other countries. For example, if the Slovenian central bank hikes interest rates, transportation costs in the country will rise. Slovenia is a key Balkan route for goods into the neighboring EU country Italy and therefore an important trade route. Higher costs of goods means lower profits, so investors would look very carefully before putting capital into Slovenian enterprises.

This is especially the case in small countries such as Bosnia, Serbia, Kosovo, Armenia, Georgia, and some of the smaller African states. They will almost certainly lack the productive capacity to manufacture or grow everything that consumers need or want. Conversely, those who are efficient at producing or manufacturing will almost certainly want at some point to become a supplier of their product to other countries.

Journalists therefore need to look beyond their own beats and countries for news. By widening their view, they also will be able to identify stories that they had not previously considered.

What Journalists Need to Know in a Global Economy

Beginning with economic activity, journalists within these smaller countries should know where and how their country trades with other countries, especially their neighbors. For example

- Who are the most important trading partners?
- Where are those trading partners located?
- What products is a country able to export?
- What products does a country need to import?
- Are there government policies that encourage or discourage exports or imports to or from certain places or involving certain products?

Like corruption, trade barriers generally lead to economic inefficiency. That doesn't mean that governments don't have good reasons for adopting them; but when they do adopt them, there is likely to be some cost: identifying that cost and who is paying it can make for good economic stories.

To some extent policy makers generally coordinate their actions with the actions of key trading partners—or they should. If they don't, they run the risk of making decisions that are undermined or weakened by a trading partner. To give a straightforward example, there is no point in raising taxes on specific goods if consumers will simply drive across the border and buy them at a cheaper price. Business and economic activity is full of similar cases.

At the level of policy making, officials can also be measured against their counterparts in other countries. International investors are almost certainly doing this and journalists should be doing it as well. For example

- Why does one country attract more foreign investment than another?
- Is policy part of the explanation?
- Why does a business make more money manufacturing a product in one country than in a neighboring one?
- Are business costs too high?

Such questions, of course, go well beyond just government policy. Journalists should be attuned to such issues and look for opportunities to explain. The general level of education, for example, may make it more appealing to open a factory in one country than another, or even in one region of a single country than another. Union and other labor practices can have a similar effect.

■ **Note**   Journalists should note that what is true of governments and policy is also true of businesses and often of labor. Company managers have to be aware of opportunities to cut costs by producing elsewhere or to boost sales by opening sales offices elsewhere. And when one company does it, all its competitors have to decide whether they should be taking similar steps.

The Relevance of Globalization

Business and economics and capital don't stand still. Relative advantages and disadvantages are constantly shifting, sometimes in very short periods of time. The attraction of depositing money in any specific country can disappear overnight if another country raises interest rates. One country's government debt may become much easier or harder to sell if another country's government debt rating is changed for the worse or better.

Behind the scenes, as all this activity is taking place, pressure is being put on governments, policy makers, company managers, labor leaders, and others to be flexible. Businesses may face many of these challenges, but they don't necessarily like it and won't be shy about asking the government to protect them. Labor leaders, seeing a risk to jobs, may become more accommodating in negotiations or they may seek legislation to protect those jobs. Policy makers have to be responsive to political pressure even when that leads to decisions that are economically shortsighted or just wrong.

Journalists both benefit and suffer from this reality. The benefit is that it offers a wide range of stories to be written or broadcast. When they start looking at their own domestic environment in comparison to other countries where things work differently, they suddenly see stories that they hadn't considered before. The suffering comes from the need for journalists themselves to become much more knowledgeable about things they previously ignored.

J

A MENTAL EXERCISE

Some experienced journalists sharpen their skills by playing a game with themselves. Imagine being caught on a plane with a government official, or a central banker, or even a company executive from another country. What questions would they ask? By going through this mental exercise of formulating questions for officials and executives from other countries, they develop a better understanding of the relevance of globalization to their own country. And hopefully they get more and better stories.

Foreign Affairs and Their Consequences Make for a Good Story

As an example of foreign affairs and their consequences, consider one Balkan country, which has a real problem in the diplomatic community. Often, its diplomatic personnel are left off guest lists of receptions held by other embassies, where serious trade business is often conceived, because a larger neighbor refuses to be present if they are there.

In this case, the larger neighbor is trying to become a member of the EU. Obviously, concern for its citizens' welfare takes a back seat to traditional enmities. Thereby lies a tale in itself.

But often the governments of emerging economies can be a bit self-centered about their own policies based on a desire to play the big stage before using a smaller platform to boost their economy and standing.

There is a wine in the Balkan states that wins rave reviews from critics. The producers make great efforts to place this wine in overseas embassies and consulates. Small producers have joined forces to try and get an overseas market. Yet their government is so busy trying to stride the big global stage that there has been little or no help for these wine producers to launch their product abroad.

■ **Note**   As you will remember from earlier comments, wine was among my specialty subjects as a business journalist, so I admit that I have an ax to grind about this particular issue. Nonetheless, I have dug up enough facts to start either an enterprise or investigative story that can be brought to a conclusion with a bit more work.

But why haven't the nation's journalists picked up this particular ball and run with it? Your reaction might be that it is a small story, not too worthy of media attention. However, all stories are worthy of attention when they can produce useful information for readers.

But be that as it may, this is a region that has almost half of its labor force in agriculture, has an unemployment rate nudging 50%, a third of the population below the poverty line, and a trade gap of a couple of billion dollars. The grape they produce is very juicy, but to a business journalist, this economic data should be even juicier.

There are some very good stories to be investigated on the basis of these facts and an opportunity for enterprising business journalists to ask serious questions of their authorities about trade policy, economic policy, trade and industry issues, and a whole host more.

A Wealth of Potential Stories

I was training some journalists in London from these regions on one occasion and some of them complained that in the UK media, they could find little or no news about their own countries. Part of the answer was that there was little or no serious news about their countries in their own newspapers.

A good journalist only has to scratch the surface and a host of stories come bursting out. Lazy journalism, protocol journalism, fearful journalism: they have no place in the bag of tricks that a good, serious, and innovative reporter should have.

There are stories everywhere. Many of them are global stories, but international stories often reflect conditions in your own country, so looking abroad is not such a bad way of helping to focus on domestic issues.

Look abroad. There's a wealth of material for good solid business and economic tales, which can also trigger home-based stories. It just takes a bit of effort, that's all!

Key Points

Reporters must

- Look beyond their own countries to put economic stories in context.

- Examine government policies carefully to see how they affect prosperity or recession.

- Look at business strategies to rate a company's success factor.

Stock and Bond Markets

Most major cities have stock exchanges, with the biggest located in New York, London, Tokyo, and Singapore. They are simply a market for buying and selling, like many of the street markets in London, especially the famous Portobello Road market in Notting Hill, where stall holders sell anything from a cabbage to an antique statue.

But the commodity in stock markets is company shares, the sale or trade of which is designed to raise capital for a company.

Business media is very important to the operation of stock markets. When companies are publicly owned—that is, when shares are held by investors outside the company—legislation demands full and open disclosure of financial information. Companies depend on media to report these accounts and information about enterprises to satisfy a shareholder's (investor's) legal right to know what is going on in the business. Of course, media reports are a transparent way of keeping everyone with a vested interest informed about company activities, especially financial information. So important is this relationship that the stock exchanges use the media to reveal sensitive company information that might affect a company's share price. The exchanges announce the "news" at exactly the same time to all media to ensure no investor gets any financial advantage over another.

Shares, Stocks, and Bonds

Shares are also known as securities. Stocks are known as equity securities and bonds are known as debt securities.

Stocks are traded on a stock exchange and in some ways are the glamour instruments of the financial markets because massive companies such as Ford, British Airways, IBM, and Google are traded there and they conjure up visions of products we can all touch and feel.

Bonds, or debt securities, are far less glamorous because they are on a "paper" market, a market where money is borrowed and lent. But it is a no less important market, with an estimated value globally of more than $80 trillion.

Bonds reach into many avenues of business and finance, with numerous governments raising cash through debt instruments such as the US Government's Treasury Bonds.

Some bonds are traded through formal "exchanges," but mostly bonds are bought and sold through brokers. Because of the size of the market, deals are mostly transacted between governments (and to a lesser extent big companies) and pension funds, banks, and mutual funds.

Local Events Spur International Market Consequences

Perhaps one of the lessons to be learned from the Julius Reuter story (described earlier in this book) is that events that are happening thousands of miles away can have an impact on what happens in local towns and cities. The business journalist must be aware of general international news and try to determine if events will have an impact on his or her local business, local community, and local citizenry.

As an example, in the mid 1990s a huge hurricane devastated the coast of the southeastern United States. Its power was terribly destructive. The first impact of that hurricane was that the citrus fruit crops of the area were destroyed, leading to a sharp jump in the global price of fruit such as oranges and lemons.

But the real international consequence that had an effect on millions of communities was that insurance payouts for the damage ran into billions of dollars. Therefore the biggest global insurance market, Lloyds of London, was forced to increase insurance premiums. This in turn meant that the cost of insuring such things as freight ships and tankers increased, so the shipping lines had to increase their costs. Suddenly, because of an act of nature, world prices for basic commodities soared, and the cost of everyday items in shops across the globe rose sharply.

This of course added to inflationary fears, so governments had to act and capped inflation by increasing interest rates. And an increase in interest rates affects anyone who has a bank account, a mortgage, or has borrowed money for any reason. As you can see, a local storm had far-reaching consequences on a huge number of individuals.

▨ **Note**   In fairness, even senior international business journalists didn't at first pick up the enormity of the consequences of the storm. But it can be seen that being a business journalist needs in-depth thinking, in-depth skills, and an exceptional ability to try to see how major global events will affect the lives of ordinary people in their own area.

Stock Exchanges, Bond Markets, and Foreign Exchange Markets

Stock exchanges (or stock markets) are the most common markets, until quite recently marked by the hubbub, arm waving, and shouting of traders on the floor of the exchange, trading a variety of shares in a whole range of businesses with shares open for sale to the public. (These shares are known as financial instruments.) Other important markets are bond markets, trading in "debt," and currency markets known as foreign exchanges (Forex). They deal in the trade of almost all national currencies such as dollars for sterling, euros for Japanese yen, or rubles for Nigerian naira.

The biggest financial exchanges are usually based in the biggest financial centers. New York is the most important stock exchange, followed by Tokyo, London, and the joint European exchange Euronext based in Amsterdam. Hong Kong and Shanghai are the important exchanges in Southeast Asia next to Tokyo.

The good business journalist will explore in depth the workings of the markets, which include the following:

- Securities such as equity and stocks
- Commodities such as wheat, coffee, copper, or sugar
- Debt such as bonds, banknotes, or debentures
- Precious metals
- Oil/ petroleum
- And the more complex trading in derivatives, futures, options, and swaps

Also, as noted, there is the foreign exchange market. Billions of dollars, pounds, euros, and other currencies change hands each day on foreign exchanges. This is a market dear to every traveler, tourist, and holidaymaker because it dictates the value of money for shopping overseas on any particular day.

But the major players in Forex are the central and commercial banks, hedge funds, securities exchanges, and institutional investors, which need to know the relative values of a currency for their trading activities. Perhaps the most significant difference between trading on Forex and other markets is that these trading centers stay open 24 hours a day.

Stock exchanges have a set trading day. For instance, The New York Stock Exchange has an opening and closing bell. But because floor trading has been taken over by electronic trading and because stock exchanges have mushroomed around the world, stocks are not far behind currencies in being traded continuously.

The best way to understand how these markets work is to report on them. But to do that, knowledge can be gained by spending time in a brokerage or commercial bank, getting to know staff economists and analysts, and asking them a thousand questions.

There are many books about trading and the various markets, and a new reporter might want to read up on how markets operate. But like journalism itself, the best way is to "do it" and gain firsthand knowledge from a working expert. Try to establish a good relationship with an economist or trader. Talk to him or her and use these analysts as useful tools. They don't mind and much prefer to help journalists understand the markets rather than get poor and inadequate stories.

These make up the financial markets and it behooves the competent business journalist to study them carefully and in some detail.

For the moment, I am examining stock and bond markets, as these are the staple items for most business reporters.

The Language of Financial Markets

Some terms used in financial markets can be confusing. So my exhortation to study these markets carefully should not go unheeded.

Briefly, a security is an asset that can be traded, on or off a formal exchange. These are also known as financial instruments.

Remember these two terms well: *securities* and *financial instruments*. While you are covering a story at a brokerage or bank, the chances are that the people you are talking to will lapse into jargon or market speak. They won't know they are doing it. They will forget that you are a journalist, not a market expert, and often you will be too shy or awkward to ask just what the hell they are talking about.

Don't be shy in asking for an explanation. Mostly people in financial markets are only too happy to explain even the most rudimentary issues in clear language, if asked. What they do get upset about is the reporter who uses "buzz words" such as "leverage" or "arbitrage" without having the faintest idea what those terms mean.

Note   I reiterate, financial journalists must be accurate and that accuracy depends on being able to enter into an intelligent conversation about an issue without trying to prove you know everything.

The Role of Stock Markets

Stock markets (or stock exchanges) are in many countries an important measure of the economic health of businesses in those countries. And the economic health of businesses in any country is often a good indicator of the economic health of the country itself. A stock market is essential to the growth of businesses and to the creation of employment and wealth.

Businesses raise capital for expansion of their activities by selling new shares to a wide public via the stock market. The investors buying the shares need to know they can get their money back again in the future by selling the shares on the stock market. They will not buy the shares in the first place unless they are confident there is an efficient stock market where the shares will be traded and through which they can sell the shares in the future at a fair price.

So stock market activity produces at least two things that journalists need to report on:

- The markets allocate capital both in the initial issuing of shares by a company and in subsequent trading of those shares.

- The markets offer an opportunity for investors of all types to demonstrate their views about the future prospects of companies by buying shares in companies they think will make good profits.

In some cases, stock markets serve other purposes. For example, in many emerging economies, governments use privatizations to make shares available to citizens. The idea is often to get the citizens to start thinking about how to manage their own wealth and to prepare for their own future costs.

By ensuring that citizens can buy a large percentage of the shares in a privatized company, the government hopes to create a share-owning culture that will be generally supportive of private enterprise.

Regulation and Transparency in Stock Markets

Effective regulation of the stock market is crucial to all of the above. If the market seems to be working on behalf of a few, well-connected individuals, it will not be able to efficiently allocate capital. Many investors will be wary because of the risk of investing in something that doesn't follow rules, and governments are unlikely to stimulate widespread interest in owning shares.

AN EXAMPLE OF SLOPPY REGULATION

A classic example of sloppy regulation came when Russia decided to opt for free market principles rather than a centrally controlled and planned economy in the early 90s. The government decided to give each citizen coupons, redeemable in shares in state enterprises as they were privatized.

A few dubious individuals immediately offered to buy these coupons from the general public, at much less than their true value; and as a result, instead of citizens owning the companies, a few oligarchs became very rich.

What's more, when trading began on the Russian stock markets, the regulations were so lax that shares were sold many times over, so that ownership of a share meant nothing because several more people might, and often did, also own the same share. So a company that issues a thousand shares had 10,000 people owning them.

There was chaos for a number of years.

Journalists should therefore be well informed of the regulatory requirement in any given country and be able to draw comparisons to best practice elsewhere. Transparency will be one of the key elements of good regulation. Listed companies should be required to release regular financial information about their performance and their risk, and they should be releasing it to everybody at the same time. If anybody is getting such information before others, then the market is working on behalf of the few against the interest of the many.

Transparency and other elements of good regulation add up to protection of shareholder rights. Shareholders own companies, and governments and regulators should be protecting those rights. The rules by which shareholders can urge changes in management at a company or even by which they can vote should be clearly spelled out. Minority shareholders should have the same rights as majority shareholders. Boards of directors should be working for the shareholders rather than for the company management.

Even well-established stock markets often fall foul of the preceding rules, but their failure only emphasizes the importance of them.

The Role of the Journalist Who Covers the Stock Market

In addition to regulation, journalists will usually be reporting on two aspects of market activity:

- They will be covering the company as it seeks to list on the exchange (issue shares for sale).

- They will be covering the day-to-day trading that re-values every listed company again and again as the trading day continues.

When a company lists for the first time, it is seeking to raise capital that might otherwise be going elsewhere: to other companies, into a loan, or real estate, to name just a few possibilities. Journalists will therefore want to tell their viewers and readers why the company wants the money and what the opportunities and risks are of buying its shares. To make their case for capital, the company should be releasing a detailed prospectus about its plans, challenges, opportunities, and so on. Such a prospectus will be a treasure chest of valuable information about the company and should allow the journalist to draw comparisons to other, similar companies.

Once listed, the company's shares are constantly trading on the exchange—or they should be, if there is enough liquidity. Efficient exchanges require good *liquidity*, a term that essentially means there will always be a buyer for anybody who wants to sell his or her shares. The price of a company's shares is always moving, a sign that the market never sets a final value on it: the value is always changing.

In this constant reassessment of what a company is worth, journalists have a chance to write stories about opportunities or threats to the individual company, to the sector it is in, to the economy generally, and even to the stock exchange itself.

Participants in the exchange, whether they are financial institutions or individuals, are the sources for this constant assessment. Uncovering their motives in deciding to buy and sell is a big part of the task of any market journalist.

The reason in part is that many others in the market want to understand why others are making decisions. Market participants often move in packs. When one investor executes a trade, others simply follow. Within the market itself, therefore, there is an appetite for news that describes what is going on in the market. Outside investors will be just as interested in knowing what the professionals think.

STOCK EXCHANGES ARE IN COMPETITION WITH EACH OTHER

In many countries, the exchange is itself a listed company whose shares can be bought and sold. The exchange will compete against another exchange in the same or a different country. Just as one company will compete against a rival making the same product, the exchange competes against rivals to list companies and to attract investors. Those exchanges that do best are themselves rewarded with a higher valuation by investors.

■ **Note** For exchanges to work well, they often need a professional infrastructure. Analysts emerge to scrutinize companies; brokers are established to sell shares to retail investors, and others; financial institutions open trading desks; companies establish investor relations' staff; and of course journalists circulate the information that comes from all of them, as well as the companies themselves.

As I've stated previously, it is not my purpose in this book to go into great detail on what a reporter should consider in viewing the activities of stock exchanges. But they should examine the roles of regulators and market practitioners worldwide to understand the most suitable models for their own countries in establishing successful stock markets; they must examine how stock exchanges work in emerging economies and be absolutely sure of the relationship between stock markets (and other financial and commodity markets for that matter) and media.

Fascinating stories can come from studying the building of a stock exchange system from the bottom up, including the evolution of computer trading and news distribution systems; the role of exchanges and development of Europe-wide markets; as well as the role of the regulator, importance of transparency, and the proper dissemination of market information.

Reporters must also weigh the balancing by market practitioners of the needs of investors, quoted companies and the regulator, the role of authorized news services, and their relationship with the market and the regulator. Business journalists must also be sensitive to financial public relations and the links it provides to financial newswires, newspapers, and broadcasters.

The following are important points that a business reporter must look at in relation to stock and financial markets:

- How modern markets have been built from scratch as opposed to those that evolved from the coffee houses of the 18th century

- The economic benefits of stock markets

- The analyst's role in the function of the stock exchange
- How the market actually functions
- Getting to know the workings of a market by talking to experts about what dealing costs and settlement are
- How money is raised in the market
- What trading systems are and how they work
- How the financial community, including journalists, cope with a market crash

It is unfortunate that electronic trading has taken over from the "Open Outcry" in which traders would sometimes resort to fisticuffs on the trading floor to win an order. But just because the fierce competition between dealers and exchanges isn't as obvious any more doesn't mean that it has disappeared.

Stock markets are fascinating enterprises, trading billions of dollars worth of stock in any given day. Reporting on stocks means reporting on great industrial names and what they are doing to retain their competitive edge: Microsoft, Cunard, Shell, AT&T—romantic names in the industrial world.

By reporting on stock exchanges, reporters get to delve into the inner workings of these big listed companies, their trials and tribulations, their shareholder revolts, and their chief executives' hiring and firing.

It's an exciting world to be part of, and I would ask, "Could a business journalist ask for anything more?"

Key Points

- Companies depend on business media to report accounts and information about enterprises to satisfy a shareholder's legal right to know what is going on in the business.
- Journalists should be well informed of the regulatory requirement in any given country and be able to draw comparisons to best practice elsewhere.
- Movement on the stock exchange can give a reporter clues to a company's health.

CHAPTER

17

Commodities and Other Exotic Financial Products

The small town of Barkerville is located some 400 miles from the major city of Vancouver in the interior of the Canadian Province of British Columbia. Its itinerant population today is about 200; and it is essentially a tourist town with dance hall girls, a hanging judge, and historic buildings. Visitors can also pan for gold.

And that's how Barkerville was born. A prospector named Billy Barker struck gold in 1860 and the inevitable gold rush began. Barkerville sprang from nothing to a population of 5,000, making it a fairly large town in those days.

As so often happened when gold fever struck, early miners in Barkerville made a lot of money. But it was the real commodity merchants who made a killing, selling pound bags of flour for $1.25 (around $30 today) as well as beans, meat, and dried fruit at the same price.

Guess who got rich.

Today's Gold Market

The romance surrounding gold has almost gone from the days when bandits robbed trains and remote wild western banks were held up by masked gunmen on horseback.

Although gold is still popular for jewelry as an adornment, in market terms, it is bought mainly as a hedge against inflation: a bit dull. The romance that once surrounded this precious metal has largely disappeared, although romantics such as Ian Fleming get the adrenalin rushing through the veins with novels such as the James Bond "baddie" Goldfinger.

The gold market does still have its moments, however. In 2013, heavy selling took place without a solid explanation, and the market panicked. Everyone tried to sell their gold holdings, thus driving the price down.

But that is rare, and although this precious metal bears reporting on, it fails to replicate its exciting beginnings and is considered a stable commodity in modern markets.

Gold is still seen as solid backup to more volatile investments. Tough economic times see the sale of gold rise. In better economic times, buyers fall away to buy products with faster returns and the gold market settles down again into a less bountiful mood. Gold still captures the imagination, but reporters following the market are more likely to see gold as an economic indicator than as an interesting commodity in itself. Nonetheless, gold is a rare precious metal that figures significantly in the commodity sector. It provides support to central banks and financial markets because of its rare and less volatile features.

Following gold on the market is really part of following a set of financial indicators. It is more of a signpost than a driver. But journalists should track it nevertheless because the major banks watch its price carefully to test the validity of what action they are considering to take in overall economic activity.

What Is a Commodity?

There are many kinds of commodities, but they are generally put into three main categories. These are energy, metals, and agriculture.

A commodity needs to be tradable—in other words, it must have substance so that it can be delivered, such as cocoa, wheat, or tin. A commodity must also have buyers—that is, it must be in demand, the factor that drives the price of commodities on the open market.

Stepping back in time for a moment and at the beginning of this book, I explained how Reuters became the information giant that it is today through its founder Julius Reuter setting the price of corn in London based on the abundance or otherwise of wheat crops on the Russian Steppes and producing the information via carrier pigeons. This was an early example of how commodity prices were set by supply and demand.

Oil as a Commodity

At about the same time that Billy Barker was panning for gold, a much less heralded but perhaps much more significant event took place about 5,000 miles away in Britain.

Coal was a hugely important commodity in the 19th century, mostly extracted from deep under the earth by hand from pits or mines. In 1847 a chemist named James Young invented a process for distilling paraffin from oil seepages at a mine, which he refined for using in miners' lamps. The residue, thicker oil—known to this day as "crude"—he used for lubricating machinery. Two years later, Abraham Gesner in Canada made a similar discovery and called his product kerosene. These two men produced the fuel that today accounts for about 90 percent of the power needs of transport vehicles: refined oil.

OIL AS A LEADING COMMODITY

There are two basic forms of oil: crude oil, which is the black stuff that comes directly from the ground or under the sea, and petroleum, which is refined oil, popularly known as gas in the United States and petrol in the UK. Petroleum is extremely important to the global economy. For example, it comprises 40 percent of total energy consumption in the United States, and many other things are derived from petroleum, such as industrial chemicals and by-products. So black gold has replaced yellow shiny gold as one of the world's most important commodities.

Oil in the Headlines

While oil managed to get a relatively placid start in life, unlike gold, it is now known as "black gold." In modern times, oil spawns news stories almost daily and most are far more dramatic than the stagecoach robber of the gold fever era.

Oil has instead given rise to pollution stories, as huge supertankers travel the world, carrying vast loads of oil. More often than is environmentally desirable, a tanker hits the rocks in bad weather, spilling its cargo and causing extensive damage to wildlife, natural environments, and communities of humankind who dwell on the coast. The Exxon Valdez disaster off the coast of Alaska was a major story in 1989, sending vast quantities of oil pouring onto the American coastline (some estimates put the figure at 11 million US gallons), and more recently the very damaging 2010 BP disaster in the Gulf of Mexico in which almost five million barrels (210 million gallons) gushed into the sea and onto the shore, causing huge harm to the environment.

The Exxon Valdez disaster in turn triggered major insurance stories because these ships and their cargo are underwritten by the biggest insurance market in the world, Lloyd's of London. Lloyd's pays for many of its insurance activities through a vehicle called "names." Names are groups of individuals who insure these ships through personal investment, tempted by large profits. The Valdez disaster saw Lloyds call in the "names" investments, bankrupting many wealthy people around the globe.

There are many other stories triggered by oil. Aircraft stories are a regular item, from helicopters transferring workers from oil rigs that are located way out to sea to the development of jet engines that reduce pollution of the atmosphere.

Piracy stories are numerous in which bandits from relatively lawless countries hijack tankers from small boats loaded with machine guns and hi-tech weaponry. Pipelines, which carry oil across vast distances, are a favorite with journalists because there is always some group or other tapping into the line and siphoning off the oil, or terrorists sabotaging a pipeline to try to wreck an economy.

Kidnappings, especially in the Niger Delta, take place by groups who hold workers, mostly foreign, for ransom and on some occasions they have executed them. Then there are bitter disagreements between states such as Belarus, Ukraine, and Russia across which pipelines carry oil, for nonpayment of bills for both gas and oil.

Some historians say, and with some evidence, that wars such as the Iraq war to depose President Saddam Hussein are really wars about who controls oil reserves.

So the formerly placid oil provides journalists with many, many news stories, not all of them linked to the markets and economies.

Oil is a commodity that spawns specialist reporters. These scribes watch carefully for events that will send the price of oil surging either up or down. This volatility is most important to all economies. As oil prices rise, so do the prices of many industrial products. Manufacturing costs soar, transport costs jump, and even home heating becomes more expensive.

The price of oil can be dictated by oil-producing countries artificially driving up the price by cutting back on output. This can be as much for political reasons as market forces. Producing countries have sometimes cut back on production to weaken the economies of nations with whom they have a dispute. On other occasions, producers have put the brakes on falling prices because national income has dropped as a result of a glut of oil on world markets.

The Struggle to Control Oil

Oil is also often the cause of power struggles, both military and economic— and, hence, a cause for more stories on oil.

The top three oil-producing countries are Russia, Saudi Arabia, and the United States. Of these, Middle Eastern countries have the lion's share. Some 80 percent of the world's reserves are located in the Middle East.

Saudi Arabia has in the main been friendly to the West, but from time to time it caps its output, limiting the amount of oil it will pump from the ground at any one time, pushing up prices, and sending shivers through Western economies that are so dependent on the commodity.

Output is largely dictated through a Vienna-based organization known as OPEC, the Organization of Petroleum Exporting Countries, and is measured in "barrels" per day. Formed in 1960 by five of the big oil exporters, OPEC now numbers 12 nations with a permanent secretariat in Austria.

OPEC meets regularly with the expressed purpose of keeping oil prices stable. Although this is largely true, oil prices have bounded up and down like a yo-yo over the years. It is largely because Saudi Arabia is a key OPEC member that oil prices, although increasing steadily, have been kept relatively stable.

There are alternative sources of oil through extraction processes, for instance, from shale, a process known as "fracking" (hydraulic fracturing). But these are expensive processes, and the main source of oil is from drilling wells below the earth's surface and pumping it out.

Britain and the United States also produce crude oil from under the sea from drilling stations called oil rigs.

THE PRICE OF GAS VERSUS THE PRICE OF CRUDE OIL

Be careful not to tie the price of gasoline at the roadside pumping stations too tightly to the price of crude oil. Once crude oil has been pumped to the surface, it needs to be refined into petroleum. Many countries don't have an extensive refining capacity and need to send crude abroad to be turned into fuel for motor vehicles. Weather vagaries, industrial disruptions, cartel combinations, and political events can diminish refining capacity. Hence the price of a gallon of gas often has little to do with the price of crude oil.

Petroleum is vital to many industries and is of major importance to the heavily industrialized economies of the globe and thus a critical concern to many nations. According to the International Energy Agency, the world at large consumes more than 30 billion barrels of oil per year, and the top oil consumers largely consist of developed nations.

Oil Trading

Oil is traded on two major exchanges: the London-based International Petroleum Exchange, now known as ICE Futures, and NYMEX, the New York Mercantile Exchange, which also deals in a wide range of other commodities from coffee to iron ore. ICE has also expanded its range of products, dealing in swaps and futures. One other important commodities exchange is Chicago Mercantile Exchange. This exchange leans more toward agricultural products but has spread its wings to become an important international enterprise.

Precious Metals as a Commodity

I now go back to real gold. Gold and precious metals are traded on similar exchanges. In London, the London Metals Exchange is the major player, closely followed by NYMEX in New York, Zurich in Switzerland, and the ancient trading location of Hong Kong.

The silver market is interesting because of extrinsic factors that may drive it. Silver prices can be affected by drought or crop blight in tea- or cotton-producing countries, especially India. India traditionally uses silver for gifts and jewelry at times of national celebrations. If the cotton or tea crop fails (which are commodities in themselves), workers have no money to purchase these items and so demand slumps.

Journalists should watch out for this sort of factor, which can be a different, if unexpected, element in the global precious metals market. Interesting commodity stories are made of such.

The Diamond Market

One last market that is exciting is the diamond market.

Diamonds are still a "girl's best friend" and are bought for cosmetic purposes. But there is also an industrial diamond used in drilling ventures because it is hard and almost indestructible.

There are a number of centers in the world that "cut and polish" diamonds, making them the attractive commodity favored by the human race. Producing more than half the "cut diamond" global output, the Belgian city of Antwerp is the acclaimed diamond capital of the world, closely followed by Amsterdam.

There is a huge supply of diamonds in the world, but the supply is carefully controlled by major companies such as the South African mining enterprise DeBeers. Russian supplies come second in volume.

There has been a big trade in diamonds on the black market, especially from countries in Africa suffering social and political upheaval.

To ensure this supply of diamonds didn't rock the market, the main producers formed the International Diamond Council, which has the task of trying to lessen the impact of "conflict diamonds."

But whenever conflict breaks out in diamond-producing countries, business journalists should pay attention to the size of the conflict and the production figures for diamonds. Either the market will be flooded because "rebels" seize mines to raise funds, or the market rises because legitimate governments jealously protect their source of income.

Agriculture

Agricultural products are also an important commodity. An estimated 40 percent of the world's surface is used to grow crops and feed livestock. Products such as grains (wheat, oats, barley), soybeans, oilseeds, livestock, dairy products, lumber, coffee, sugar, and cocoa all fall under the agricultural commodities banner.

According to the International Labour Organization, more than one billion people are involved in global agriculture. And steadily increasing world populations continue to push the demand for food upward.

Agriculture gives rise to a wide variety of stories: famine, hunger riots, and plant and animal diseases. More recently, the development of genetically modified foods (super foods) has become a controversial topic, with many scientists arguing these foods can safely ease starvation; while opponents, which are often governments, fearing these modified crops can be harmful to the human body: another great source of stories.

Those reporters who prefer to follow companies on the stock exchange will also reap benefits from these diverse views, as production and sales of new fertilizers and pesticides improves company share prices, while the fate of major chemical companies such as Monsanto, Syngenta, and Bayer, the main producers of genetic foods, fight off the critics of their products and try to achieve both acceptance and increases in sales.

Agriculture also triggers environmental stories, as farmers cut into rain forests to increase growing capacity while animal welfare organizations fight to protect endangered species such as lions, tigers, leopards, and bears.

Reporting on Commodities

All those commodities—oil, gold, silver, and diamonds—have a glamour and excitement about them that makes reporting on them glamorous in itself.

Now comes the tricky part for business and financial journalists: steering one's way through the other *exotic financial instruments*. To combat this, I followed my own advice and maintained close contact with a market expert whom I regularly called for help when the word *derivative* cropped up.

Derivatives embrace market trading methods known as *futures contracts, swaps,* and *exchange-traded commodities*—all traded on commodities exchanges. Futures or forward contracts are probably the easiest to understand.

A *forward or futures contract* is an agreement between two parties to buy a commodity at a price fixed at the time of the deal but to be paid at some time in the future. The buyer and seller are to all intents and purposes guessing that the price of the commodity will be either greater or smaller than when the transaction actually takes place. The practice of *hedging* is associated with these deals, enabling a buyer to trade in the same commodity at a different price or cut his or her losses if the futures contract goes wrong. For example, wheat traders might hedge against a poor harvest by agreeing to buy or sell wheat elsewhere at a lower price.

Swaps are a similar type of deal in which cash is the commodity. Used widely in the bond market, a dealer might agree to swap the interest paid on a bond for its market price, but again as a future trade.

Traders find these concepts simple; journalists in the main don't. So my advice remains: ask a person who knows or even take a course in this kind of trading. It is hard to understand but easy to get wrong, something no financial journalist can afford to do.

Key Points

- A commodities exchange is an exchange where various commodities and derivatives are traded.

- Most commodity markets across the world trade in agricultural products and other raw materials and contracts based on them.

- Oil and other commodities can give rise to many different types of stories. Watch these commodities carefully—especially oil.

- Ask an expert about derivatives. Analysts and traders think they're simple. I do not!

Investigating Company Accounts and Assessing the Board

Successful businesses become and remain successful mainly because they have a board of directors who are knowledgeable, honest, and hardworking.

A director's main responsibility is to the company shareholders and employees. In this capacity, a director is required by law to keep company records, file them regularly with the tax authorities, and follow the legal trading requirements of the country or countries in which the enterprise does business. A board of directors, jointly and severally, must make sure the company's accounts are a "true and fair view" of the business's finances.

To fulfill these obligations, directors draw up annual accounts, which are a profile of a company's financial health, profitable undertakings, and honest dealings.

Business journalists who have even an elementary understanding of the role of directors and can review a set of accounts have a signpost to stories about business success and growth; malpractice, such as corrupt activities; labor relations—good or otherwise; and indications about how well a business is handling the speed of change in the modern world.

These make for vital and exciting stories for every member and sector of society.

Reviewing a Company's Annual Accounts

In most Western countries, company annual accounts are filed with a regulator. The rules and regulations can be quite complicated, but the requirement is that basic information be available to the public on such things as ownership, location, trading features, and so forth.

All registered companies—that is, limited liability companies—need to file annual returns. A set of company accounts must be filed with the returns. But unlimited partnerships and sole traders, while obliged to file a return, do not have to file an audited set of accounts. So if a company is a company protected by law as a limited liability business, it must produce annual accounts according to local law and make them available to the public.

But how can journalists tell if the accounts are reliable and accurate? In looking at the accounts of any company, large or small, journalists should first look to see if those accounts have been audited and what the auditor's review says.

HOW TO ACCESS ANNUAL ACCOUNTS

In the UK, journalists can get the accounts of almost all companies trading in the country through a government agency called Companies House. For a small fee, details are available of a company's accounts audited and registered by the company, usually through its accountants. All of this information is accessible to the public for a fee of £1 per document.

In the United States, there are two similar organizations. One is the Public Company Accounting Oversight Board (PCAOB), which oversees the audits of public companies; and the other is the Securities and Exchange Commission (SEC), which is more of a watchdog and oversees the key players in the securities world, including exchanges, brokers, dealers, investment advisors, and mutual funds. The SEC is "concerned primarily with promoting the disclosure of important market-related information, maintaining fair dealing, and protecting against fraud."

The annual accounts should contain, at minimum, a balance sheet and a profit and loss statement. The balance sheet shows what assets and liabilities the company has and where the money came from to finance them. Major enterprises usually publish an annual report, which gives a descriptive account of the activities of a company in its previous year of trading. This report contains the annual accounts.

Beware of using such information when trying to discover how successful or otherwise a company is in an emerging economy. The rules and regulations are often not as rigid as those in the West, and it's possible for a company to cover up its true status more easily than if it was being examined by Western standards. In fact, the European Union has set regulatory reform as one of the conditions for gaining EU membership, and the United States has made the same demand of countries to which it donates substantial funds. But in some economies, progress is slow.

Understanding the Balance Sheet

Don't be afraid of balance sheets. You don't have to be an accountant to read one and get important information from it. (You might need to be an accountant to draw one up, but that's a different story!) As long as you have a reasonable level of skill in arithmetic, you should be OK.

A *balance sheet* is simply a statement of what a company owns and owes at the point the accounts were prepared. It is just an evaluation put into black and white of a company's worth. It lists the net worth of a company—all it owns, known as *assets*, and everything it owes, called *liabilities*.

■ **Note**   A sample balance sheet is given in the Appendix.

You will recall that I cautioned at the beginning of this book that the golden rule is that there is no golden rule. So there is a little glitch in this description of a company's accounts that a journalist needs to be aware of.

Liabilities can be called a credit because a loan, which will appear under liabilities, can be treated as a cash input. This is accountant-speak, but just be on your guard that you don't get fooled when interpreting a balance sheet.

A balance sheet is called a balance sheet because both sides must "balance." Assets must equal liabilities plus equity.

The information will reveal a company's income, its cash flow, and how much shareholders have contributed to the company, called *shareholders' equity*. To reiterate, assets are things that a company owns that have value, liabilities are financial items that a company owes to others, and shareholders' equity is the money that would be left if a company sold all of its assets and paid off all of its liabilities. This last item is important when calculating the value of the earnings of each share in the company based on the latest balance sheet.

A company's profit is generally stated as "pretax profit"—which means it still has to pay taxes, so the true profit has yet to be revealed.

As you review the balance sheet, be sure to watch out for notes attached to the accounts. These will give you hints about what stories to look for, because directors must reveal any items that may affect a company's performance. For example, an airline might post a healthy profit, but the footnotes will reveal that the airplane fleet is aging and needs to be replaced. That item is costly and obviously will reflect on future profits.

Now that balance sheets no longer hold terror for you, it's time to see what other information about a company you should look for.

What to Look for in Annual Accounts

The first thing to do when you get your hands on the annual accounts is to verify that the accounts have been fully audited and what the auditor's opinion says.

Next, you need to ask the following questions about the company, whose answers can be found in the company's various financial statements:

Is the company bankrupt or solvent? Look again at the balance sheet. The total assets should be greater than the total liabilities. If not, the company will not be able to carry on trading without an injection of more capital from its owners. The cash and receivables should be greater than the payables. If not, the company may not be able to pay its bills and will be forced to stop trading, unless it can borrow more money or get its owners to put in more capital.

How is the company funded? Some funding will be equity—capital put in when shares were issued plus retained profits from earlier years. Some will be long-term loans. If these loans are high in relation to equity, this could mean trouble in the future if trading and profits go down and the company cannot pay the loan interest.

Does the company have any loans? Low levels of long-term loans against equity reduce risk. Look for information about when loans will have to be repaid. If it is soon, will the company be able to make the repayments or to take out replacement loans?

Where does the company get its income? To understand a company's business, look at where it gets its income. Consider the profit and loss statement and any notes on income to see if they give any breakdown by product, market, or country. Check to see if there is anything unusual about the expenditure in the profit and loss statement and in any analysis of costs in the notes to the accounts. Do the costs relate to the activities described in the introduction and directors' report? Are they reasonable in the light of the levels of income?

Does the company have a secure asset base with which to continue its operations? Consider what the business owns—look under the list of assets—and look at the age of these assets from the depreciation calculation. This will be in the notes to the accounts and will show how the costs of long-term or "fixed" assets have been spread over their expected life. You can see how much of the original cost has been allocated to past years' income and expenditure statements. If this is a high percentage, it means the assets will need replacing soon. Will the company be able to raise the capital to buy the replacements and stay in business?

Do the assets, including property, relate to the business the company is carrying out? If the company owns assets that do not seem to be needed for the business, maybe they have been bought for the private use of the directors or other individuals.

Who is on the board of directors? Directors run the company and have a great deal of power over what it does—more so than the shareholders. Who are they? How much are they paid? Is it reasonable? Are they also directors of other companies that might be linked? Is any trading between companies with the same controlling directors on fair terms? Or is one company being deliberately favored?

How many months of revenue does the level of receivables represent? Revenue from trading is the lifeblood of a company, and sometimes directors are tempted to overstate it to exaggerate profits. Look at the level of receivables in relation to revenue. If this is higher than you would expect it to take to get customers to pay their invoices, is there a problem? Is the administration of the company failing to get prompt payment from customers, or is it possible the revenue is overstated? Will all these receivables get collected?

Who owns the company's shares? Companies are often part of a group. Look to see if the company you are examining owns shares in other companies or if its shares are owned by another company. Who is really in control? If companies in the same group are trading with each other, is it on fair terms or are there any distortions?

Can you identify any trends in the report? Trends over time are very revealing. Compare figures in the accounts to the previous year, and look to see if anything has changed significantly. Is revenue rising or falling? Are costs rising or falling in step with revenue? Has there been any big investment in new assets? Have any new loans been taken out? What are the reasons for these changes?

Is cash flow compatible with profit figures? Cash can be measured more accurately than profit, and it is harder to manipulate the reported figures. So it is a good idea to see if the cash flow and the profit figures look compatible. High profit and low cash flow could mean profits are overstated and vice versa.

Has the company made any loans? Companies can make loans to other companies or to individuals and this will show up as an asset or a receivable in the balance sheet. But apart from banks, this is an unusual thing to do. If you see such loans on the balance sheet, you should ask whether there is a good business reason for doing it.

How is the company using its profit? Profit provides dividends as a return on investment to shareholders, taxes to the government, and capital to reinvest in the business. It is a good idea to look at what is being done with the profit. Is a prudent level being retained in the business and is capital expenditure being made to sustain the business? Or is it all being distributed to the owners, putting the future of the business at risk?

Understanding the Profit and Loss Statement

Next, look at the profit and loss statement, which shows the income and the expenditure for the latest financial year. It is compiled on an *accruals basis*. That means it takes in items that are owed to the company (*receivables*) or items the company owes to creditors (*payables*), even if the cash settlement has not yet been made.

Also, look to see how the company is funded. Some funding will be *equity* (capital put in when shares were issued, plus retained profits from earlier years). Other funding will come from *long-term loans*. If these loans are high in relation to equity, this could mean trouble in the future if trading and profits go down and the company cannot pay the loan interest. This information can be found in the balance sheet.

ANNUAL REPORTS

Another source of company accounts in both the UK and the United States is a company's annual report, which is legally required from public companies and those listed on the stock exchange. Depending on the size of the company, these reports are usually glossy, well-produced documents that are sent to shareholders. Most companies make copies readily available to journalists. As noted, annual accounts are primarily bookkeeping, while annual reports are narrative.

What Journalists Need to Know about Boards of Directors

The board of directors is a group of people elected by the stockholders (the owners) to represent their interest and to protect the stockholders' investment. The directors must also ensure that investors receive a decent return on their investment. Such are the guiding principles in Western open market economies.

But journalists covering emerging democracies should be aware that open-market principles are still evolving and in some European countries, the reality is much different; directors often feel that it is their primary responsibility to protect the employees of a company first and the stockholders, or shareholders, second.

Note Government regulation on filing accounts in emerging democracies is sometimes not as rigid as those in London or New York. So care must be taken in looking at the accounts of companies in emerging democracies to ensure that the data reveals the whole story.

Usually, the board is made up of individuals. In most cases, directors have a vested interest in the company, work in upper management, or are business-savvy independents.

Directors run the company and have a great deal of power over what it does—more so than the shareholders. Therefore, it is necessary for reporters to ask such questions as the following:

- Who are the board members?

- How much are board members paid?

- Is the compensation reasonable?

- Are any board members also directors of other companies that might be linked?

- Is any trading between companies with the same controlling directors on fair terms? Or is one company being deliberately favored?

THE NON-EXECUTIVE DIRECTOR

One class of director is known as a *non-executive director* (NED). This class of director is brought in because of expertise that might help a company's operation. They are advisers rather than hands-on executives, but they have the same legal responsibilities as other directors and can be held responsible for any problems the company might have, especially financial or legal.

Asking such questions is essential to assessing the overall health of a company. For example, at the turn of the century, some executives and directors of the American energy company Enron were indicted on charges of poor financial reporting and concealing billions of dollars of company debt. They were found guilty in a district court, but the decision was later overturned.

More recently, controversy has erupted over the bonuses paid to senior executives of banks. This has been a massive debating point in many countries, but especially so in the key financial capitals of London and New York. The boards of many financial services companies have come under fire for awarding massive bonuses, usually a responsibility of the board. British bank Royal Bank of Scotland, for example, came under fire for awarding its chief executive Stephen Hester £2.2 million, which contrasted with the average pay of £34,000. The bank was taken into the public domain during the banking crisis of the late '80s, when the government took an 80 percent stake to help prevent trading problems. Lord Oakeshott, former Treasury Spokesman for UK Liberal Democrat Party, declared that bankers are "the best paid public sector workers by a mile, in a bank that keeps failing the public by failing to lend. Let's end this nonsense and nationalise RBS now."

Revenue from trading is the lifeblood of a company, and sometimes directors are tempted to overstate it to exaggerate profits. Look at the level of receivables in relation to revenue. How many months of revenue do the level of receivables represent? If this is higher than you would expect it to take to get customers to pay their invoices, is there a problem? Is the administration of the company failing to get prompt payment from customers, or is it possible the revenue is overstated? Will all these receivables get collected?

Trends over time are very revealing. Compare figures in the accounts to the previous year, and look to see if anything has changed significantly. Consider the following:

- Is revenue rising or falling?
- Are costs rising or falling in step with revenue?
- Has there been any big investment in new assets?
- Have any new loans been taken out?
- What are the reasons for these changes?

Cash can be measured more accurately than profit, and it is harder to manipulate the reported figures. So it is a good idea to see if the cash flow and the profit figures look compatible. High profit and low cash flow could mean profits are overstated and vice versa.

Covering Annual Meetings

One small note of caution: In my early days of business journalism, I couldn't get out of my head that investors were individuals, people such as me who had put a few pounds or dollars into buying some shares in a big company.

Don't ever fall into that trap.

When writing about or researching investors, remember that for big companies, the investors are big. They are mutual funds, banks, insurance companies, and other major organizations that can own thousands and thousands of shares.

Although the board can be in control of the company, major investors can bring huge influence to bear; and *annual general meetings* (AGMs) can sometimes be uncomfortable meeting places for directors if a major investor, with a big block of voting stock, is upset with their performance.

AGMs to which journalists are allowed access (there is no legal obligation on a company to grant access to reporters) can be very interesting occasions, full of conflict and controversy—that is, they are a wealth of potential stories. It's worth covering at least one AGM of a major company in your career.

In the end, keep in mind that no single financial statement or annual meeting will tell the complete story about a company's performance or even viability. But, taken in context with other information, it can provide a very powerful information source for financial journalists and produce data, which is the reporter's best tool when it comes to writing an in-depth and accurate story about any company, big or small.

Watching and analyzing the activities of companies, especially medium-to-large enterprises, from balance sheet to activities of the directors, can paint a story worth telling—a story that can detail information that would not be evident to a member of the public who can't delve into a company's background in quite the way that a business journalist can.

Key Points

- Limited and listed companies must file annual accounts with a state regulator. These accounts are available to the public.

- Company accounts contain a balance sheet: a snapshot of a company's financial situation.

- Look at a company's profit and loss statement to see its financial health.

- Understand the role and responsibilities of a company director.

- It's important to report on an annual general meeting (AGM). AGMs can help build stories.

- Criticisms of directors' bonuses are a controversial topic. Try to analyze these extra payments, perhaps with the help of a specialist.

Privatization

For more than thirty years, governments in Europe have been privatizing more and more of the activities that were previously done by the state. Eastern Europe joined this trend in the early 1990s and generally continues it today, despite exceptions in some countries and sectors. The United States has privatized a small number of state-owned enterprises in the transport and finance sector, and various US states have sold off utilities such as water and electricity.

But while privatization is often hotly debated by American politicians as a policy, American government sell-offs are drops in the bucket compared to the 130 or so enterprises sold by the UK over three decades or the French privatization program, which saw more than 50 enterprises privatized since 1990.

Part of the reason that there is a sharp difference in privatization program between the United States and other Western economies is the open-market philosophy. The United States has led the world in the policy of allowing private ownership, while governments in France, Britain, and other parts of Europe nationalized a wide range of companies in the last century and maintained control well into the 1990s. In Russia, even after perestroika and President Boris Yeltsin's market reform program, many state enterprises continued to be owned and operated by the state.

So what do these trends mean for business journalism? Why should privatization take place? What are the pros and cons of government ownership and private-sector ownership?

What Privatization Means for the Business Journalist

Business journalists need to understand the differences between an open market economy and a controlled or centrally planned economy.

The United States is the exemplar of open market policies and philosophies promulgating the ideal of economic systems with no barriers to market trading. Such systems are marked by low trade tariffs and taxation, few licensing regulations, and limitations on trade union or workers association interference in trade.

The financial and social collapse of the former Soviet Union gave huge impetus to Eastern European states to follow the American model, and broadly that is what has happened.

North Korea, on the other end, is the epitome of a closed market, with massive state control over business dealings, few if any businesses privately owned, and government managing industry.

So business journalists need to look at privatization in different ways depending on the market policies adopted in different countries. The open market is quite clear in the United States, in Britain, and other Western European countries; but in the old Eastern Europe, it is not quite so developed and governments are busy selling off their state enterprises as they try to transform their closed economies into an open market.

The Advantages of Privatization

Often, government ownership means business decisions are made for political purposes, such as job protection. This setup puts government officials in charge of reconciling conflicting interests when, usually, they are the least qualified to do so.

Although some experts would argue that there are merits to centrally planned and controlled economies in some countries at certain stages of development, generally private sector ownership brings greater economic flexibility, innovation, investment in machinery and in people, and economic growth.

For governments, the advantages of privatization are numerous. Privatization delivers income to the government from the sale of state enterprises and from future taxes paid by that enterprise, with which the government can pay for other public goods and services. Privatization moreover increases the chances that the privatized company will respond to market needs rather than political ones. It also ensures that private sector managers and shareholders carry some of the blame if things go wrong, and thereby reduces political pressures on the government. A final benefit is that it often allows governments to help create a shareholder culture among their citizens.

The Disadvantages of Privatization

While there are considerable merits to privatization, there are also draw-backs. In the case of selling utilities, for example, governments have tended to offload enterprises that were monopolies, such as water. The prime purpose, which was to raise funds for the government, was met. But because the utility was a monopoly, the advantage of lower prices and competition was lost. The utility could do what it liked; and since its remit was to make a profit, prices were uncapped, which lead to much more expensive products.

Because privatized companies are sold in an open-market environment, there is no curb on who could buy them. Several enterprises in the UK have been snapped up by overseas bidders, who have no national interest or community welfare program at the core of their objectives. They simply want to make as much profit for shareholders as possible, so public interest is a low priority.

A privatized company almost always has new management. Managers of state-run companies generally have different objectives, such as ensuring customers can buy the product at a reasonable price—one that won't embarrass the government, no matter what it costs to produce.

New management also needs to implement efficient work practices, which often means reducing the workforce. So unemployment becomes a by-product.

For example, in the UK, Prime Minister Margaret Thatcher undertook a massive program of privatization of state industries in the 1980s. Her successor, John Major, carried on that policy and set about selling off one of the last big state-owned companies, the railway system, in 1993. The railway system needed massive investment for modernization and proponents of privatization hailed a new era of railway efficiency when the government introduced legislation to sell off British Rail.

Supporters of the plan claimed, among other things, that privatization would bring improved customer service; but this aim failed to materialize in the early years because the new owners miscalculated a voluntary redundancy program for drivers, who left the privatized service in droves. Trains had to be canceled, fares were increased, and the service was deemed far worse than when under state control. There were also some railway accidents, including one that was especially serious and sapped public confidence. Critics accused the rail companies of skimping on safety to increase profits.

Alarmed at public hostility to the privatization, the government intervened on how much the companies could charge for fares and how they scheduled their train timetables.

The privatization process was beginning to unravel.

The main incentive to any buyout is to make a state industry profitable, and this was looking increasingly difficult for the investing enterprises. The critics seemed to be right. But over a couple of decades, slower than anticipated at the time of privatization, the rate of fare increases became slower than under state control, many more trains were scheduled each day, and stations had been renovated on most routes and new trains (rolling stock) purchased. Investment in rolling stock was largely based on revenue, so carriages were smaller; passengers were made to stand for long journeys, and cancellation of services became commonplace. But punctuality did not largely improve and, although passenger numbers did increase, other means of transport siphoned off some travelers from the railways.

So privatization in this instance has been a two-edged sword. But there is a consensus of thought that if the railway had been left in government hands, it would have been starved of investment cash, especially in times of economic downturns—of which there have been many in recent times—and the railways would have suffered under state control.

Hostility toward Privatization

In many countries, hostility to privatization is endemic in government itself. Politicians only introduce privatization to attract foreign government donor funds or to gain membership to political entities such as the European Union. So it is necessary for business journalists to watch the process carefully.

In Bosnia, for example, the government planned to sell off one of its tobacco factories. There was widespread international interest, as the factory had a healthy balance sheet and it was potentially a good buy.

But the Prime Minister had staked his reputation on demanding that any sell-off, a very unpopular move in the country, would ensure that extra jobs for workers would be part of the deal. As a consequence, he tied a condition to the sale that required the buyer to build a luxury hotel in a remote area where it was very unlikely the hotel would generate business. This was his idea for placating critics of privatization. The one buyer who showed interest in the tobacco plant was unwilling to invest in a white elephant and the sale fell through.

The initial loss of jobs that would have been lost at privatization would probably have been redressed with increased output from the facility, but government was unwilling to risk that.

The Role of the Press in Privatization

The press's role is as a guardian of an effective process—keeping privatizations transparent and honest and ensuring the government is demanding the best terms and getting them.

To be efficient in this role, journalists need to tap sources of information and understanding from the full spectrum of experts and stakeholders: government officials, investment bankers, lawyers, tax advisers, equity analysts, economists, consultants, "good-government" advocates, embassies, businessmen, competitors, and workers.

There are thousands of questions that journalists can—and should—ask about privatization. Some of them include

- What is the government's privatization schedule?

- Who are the government's advisers?

- What is the value of the assets of the enterprise and what are its liabilities?

- How do those assets compare to others in the same business, either in the public or the private sector?

- Is it possible to actually view the assets that are listed, in the case of a factory—for example, its plant and machinery or delivery fleet?

- Are the assets shrinking in value over the course of the privatization?

- Do all bidders have access to the same information?

- Is there a prospectus? (A *prospectus* is a document for potential investors that outlines the company's business, includes financial statements, biographies of officers and directors, their remuneration, and a list of assets.)

- What does the prospectus warn about?

- Who wins and who loses in the privatization?

- Are the bidders related to government officials in any way?

- Are bids open to the public?

- What can bidders offer besides the purchase price?

- Did the government set realistic objectives? Did it achieve them?

Just as there are thousands of questions that can be asked about privatization, there are almost as many stories to be written.

Covering the Private Sector

Capital is finite, for the private sector and for the government. If the government owns all the economic activity, it will struggle to make choices about whether to invest more into education or airlines, more into wages or research, and so on. By privatizing many businesses, the government lets consumers and producers make these choices based on supply and demand.

Journalists who have reported on state monopolies and centrally planned economies should get used to covering the private sector differently. For example, when British Airways was privatized, reporters had to switch their research and investigations by asking questions of company directors instead of government ministers. They needed to get their information from the company accounts and not the UK Treasury. They were required to report about an annual general meeting, with shareholders in attendance, sometimes asking awkward questions. So the whole approach to reporting on the privatized company shifted from dealing with government officials to approaching businesspeople and investors.

Businesses compete with one another. Decisions, therefore, have to be judged by their business rationale rather than by their political impact.

Simple actions like layoffs can make a great deal of business sense because they allow the company to compete more effectively in the market. If the company is owned by the government, such decisions are more likely to be weighed by the political impact of unemployed workers.

Businesses are primarily interested in profits; governments are primarily interested in elections. Businesses also carry out a fair number of functions that are beneficial to the economy as a whole. They train workers, invest in new capacity, advertise (thereby subsidizing entertainment), innovate, and much more.

So reporters need to view businesses sold off by the state from a whole new point of view.

Comparisons can be made between the performance of the new company and the achievements of the old:

- Does the new company give better customer satisfaction under open-market-style management than it did when it was government owned?
- Have working conditions improved?
- Are targets being met?
- Has new equipment been installed?
- Are the new work practices benefiting employees?

These are questions that can give rise to good stories, whatever the answers to such questions are.

Globally, governments are converting to open-market policies, which mean big sell-off programs of state assets. There is no guarantee that this global trend of privatization sell-offs will improve industrial performance and public services, so it is up to good business reporters to tell the stories of its successes and failures.

A Look at Balance Sheets

If journalists want to cover business activity, they need to speak the language of the businesses themselves. That means understanding company accounts, including balance sheets, cash-flow statements, and income statements. Balance sheets are in a sense devices to measure the general health of a business. The credit crisis that began in 2007 and has since spread around the world is largely a problem of balance sheets. Journalists who fail to understand them won't be able to cover the crisis with any depth.

■ **Terms**   As you've learned in previous chapters, the balance sheet measures what the company owns (the assets) and how it paid for those assets (the liabilities and the equity). The *liabilities* have to be paid back, with interest. The *equity* is the money raised by issuing shares. It is often called *risk capital* because the shareholders bear the risk if things go badly, and receive the benefits if things go well.

When journalists cover the privatization of a government-owned property, they should look at the balance sheet to assess how the company compares to others in the country and sector. One of the basic questions is whether the government is simply transferring existing shares to the public, or whether there will be a capital increase, that is, an effort to raise new funds from shareholders.

Journalists also need to ask whether the government will be selling a majority of the company and giving up control, or somehow keeping enough shares to block certain company decisions. Governments can maintain control even if they have a minority shareholding in some cases.

For example, airports in the United States, UK, and EU are popular investments in which the majority shareholding is private but where government retains a share. The rationale is that if private ownership fails, governments can step in to keep a vital transportation link working.

Private investors will almost certainly see additional risk if the government is maintaining control. It suggests the company and its managers will not be able to do some things because of market demands but will have to accommodate political considerations.

Once privatized, the company's balance sheet will to some extent determine how big it can grow, how much it will have to pay to borrow money, and even whether it is vulnerable to being bought by another company. Any given amount of equity is likely to limit how many assets a company can acquire. The company's own lenders (providers of the cash that becomes a liability) will want to see a nice equity cushion in most cases before they are willing to commit funds.

The balance sheet is also where the company records its working capital: the short-term assets and liabilities that are needed on a daily basis to pay workers, suppliers, and others and to extend credit to customers and others. The working capital management is a key responsibility of the executives and is often especially problematic in fast-growing companies.

Privatized companies will in most cases have to deal with either the capital markets or with lending institutions. Journalists should follow this interaction closely because that is where they will get a good sense of how others perceive the company. In some cases, the stock market (for listed companies) is responding to decisions that have taken place between the company and its lenders or shareholders. Journalists need to see those connections.

A Focus on the Future

Investors in private companies, whether they provide debt or equity, also tend to be very focused on the future.

They rarely take time to look back at how a company did last year or in earlier years: their concern is to forecast how the company will do next year and in subsequent years and to invest accordingly. Journalists covering such companies therefore have to be constantly seeking the management's view about the future, including its plans and worries, and its response to the dangers it anticipates.

■ **Tip** The business world is forward-looking. The journalists who cover it have to learn to think about it in the same way that the company managers do.

Privatization Agencies

In countries that are moving from a closed to open-market economy, privatization of state industries is usually managed by a quasi-government agency called a *privatization agency*. Privatization agencies usually aim to create an open economy and ownership structure, maximize investment, achieve social and political acceptability, and establish clear ownership structures.

An example is the activities of the Serbian Privatization Agency, which oversaw a relatively large sell-off of state assets: the state petroleum company, three major banks, the mobile telephone company, an airline, a hotel chain, and numerous other smaller state-owned industries.

Take a look at the benefits that accrued overall; the costs to government; the benefits and costs to investors; the benefits and costs to workers; and the benefits and costs to the company, its sector, and the broader economy. Which privatizations were successful? Which were worth investing in? Where are those companies now going?

This might seem an onerous and difficult exercise. But with a bit of research, it is possible to get a good feel for the privatization process, as Serbian companies have mostly now been sold. By applying some of the journalistic techniques outlined in this book, you can construct a good example of what privatization can mean to a country aiming for a free-enterprise environment and the stumbling blocks it faces along the way.

Key Points

- The business journalist needs to understand the key elements and importance of privatization to report on the financial health of a company or of a sector.

- It is necessary to have a basic understanding of company accounts, including the balance sheet, and what they can say about a company.

- Track important new companies on the stock exchange to assess their success.

SMEs and the Economy

Global analysts and economic commentators all agree that one of the significant characteristics of a flourishing and growing economy is a booming *small and medium enterprise* (SME) sector.

The EU definition of an SME is an enterprise that has 250 employees or less, and an annual turnover of not more than €50 million. In the range below that *medium enterprise* cutoff, a *micro enterprise* is defined as one with between one and nine employees and a turnover of less than €2 million; and a *small enterprise* is defined as one with between 10 and 50 employees and a turnover of less than €10 million.

The US definition of an SME varies according to industry and type of business, with the number employees in a medium enterprise ranging up to 1,500 but usually capping out at 500; in a small enterprise, 250; and a micro enterprise, 6.

When you buy a paper from the local corner store or even buy a hot dog on a city street, you are therefore technically a customer of an SME. More typically, the term SME in business parlance connotes companies in the medium range—from textile companies to computer and electronics firms to orchards and vineyards.

Analysts who cover this sector, supported by data from UK, US and EU government departments, say that SMEs play an extremely important role in the economic development of a country and contribute to national wealth in various ways. Not only do SMEs create employment for both rural and urban labor forces, but also they provide sustainability and innovation in the economy as a whole.

SMEs have an impact on income distribution, tax revenue, and employment, as well as on efficient utilization of resources and stability of family income. They also have a propensity to employ more labor-intensive production processes than large enterprises. Consequently, they contribute significantly to the provision of employment opportunities, the generation of income, and the reduction of poverty.

The SME sector contains such a wide variety of industries, plays such an important role in economic development, and provides so many jobs globally, that business and economic reporters need to cover it closely.

SME companies are part of macroeconomics as a sector and of microeconomics as small companies. Moreover, some SMEs grow to be large multinational corporations that are household names on the stock and bond markets, such as the examples in the sidebar. There is no greater thrill for a journalist than to find he has been reporting annually on a small enterprise that grows with each passing year until it blossoms into a listed company with wide-reaching international operations.

Reporting on SMEs is, however, mostly driven by the macroeconomic consideration that they are a sector that is important to almost every national economy in the world.

FROM SME TO HOUSEHOLD NAME

Many large enterprises had their origins as small and medium enterprises, and in many economies SMEs are the starting point toward industrialization. To understand SMEs and their importance, journalists should take a look at the origins of many of today's big companies.

There are dozens of examples of companies we know as household names today that began as SMEs. Microsoft, Apple, Amazon, and Google all began as one to three guys in a garage; Vodafone was once a little spin-off from Racal; and Hewlett-Packard started in a little wood shack.

The Development of SMEs

The impact of SMEs is far reaching. According to the EU Annual Report 2012, an estimated 23 million SMEs in the EU provide around 87 million jobs. And more than two-thirds of all jobs in the EU are in SMEs—a proportion that is on the rise.

According to 2010 U.S. census data, there are roughly 21 million enterprises with between 1 and 500 employees, numbering 60 million employees in aggregate.

In many economies, small and large firms are interlinked, which is crucial for the attraction of foreign investment. But to prosper, SMEs need a supportive business environment, adequate basic infrastructure services, access to short and long-term funding at reasonable rates, equity and venture capital, advisory assistance, and knowledge about market opportunities. They typically suffer from weak entrepreneurial skills and deficiencies in accounting, production management, and business planning.

So far, the international experience shows that very few government and donor initiatives have succeeded in implementing sustainable strategies for SME development in emerging economies. In fact, economic difficulty was far more of a spur to the development of SMEs, including one-person enterprises and small-scale businesses such as tea and coffee shops.

Nowadays it is widely deemed that a government's role in the process should be limited to providing a sound environment for private sector development, correcting potential market failures, and creating a level playing field that will allow SMEs to compete with their larger counterparts on an equal basis.

Most governments do not have the finances or the ability to get involved directly in SME financing and service provision. Government appears not to be the appropriate vehicle to implement and coordinate such efforts, and public–private partnerships for SME development seem a more critical element for the success of these efforts.

Improving Media Coverage of SMEs

How many times do reporters rush to a press conference thrown by a major industry and barely cast a glance at a press release from a little guy? That is too often the case, not only in emerging economies but in many other parts of the world. Yet they are ignoring a real economic story, which is lying under their very noses.

There are two major actions that business journalists can take to improve media coverage of SMEs. One is to do some research and match the statistics for SMEs in their own countries against those of the EU or US. Is it a similar situation, and what reporting can be done on it in both a regional and inter-national context? If the EU analysts are correct, then inward investment is directly connected to the success of small business in emerging markets. But does the outside world know about it?

▨ **Note** Some will argue that journalists report bad news. By its very definition, news is anomalous and mostly disturbing. But business reporting can draw attention to the positive. Using the reporting and news skills outlined elsewhere in this book, attractive reporting is possible on the rise of SMEs.

The other major concern for business journalists is to check if their government is living up to its stated support of the SME sector. The governments of numerous economies in transition have gone on record as saying they have helped increase economic growth through activities supporting the SME sector. "SMEs are at the top of the EU priority list. They are the engine of economic growth and job creation," says Richard Brunton, EU Minister for Jobs, Enterprise & Innovation.

A range of government statistics shows the number of SMEs globally is increasing year by year, providing new jobs. Many governments claim they have created a favorable SME environment through programs and policies such as the following:

- legal reform
- financial and investment support
- provision of credit guarantees
- assistance in creation and development of support infrastructures
- business information and consultancy support
- promotion of foreign economic activities
- support of innovation activities and introduction of modern technologies
- introduction of favorable tax policies
- vocational education and training
- creation of simplified systems for statistic reports and accountancy
- support of state purchases
- establishment of national centers for SMEs

Admittedly these programs and policies have had to weather a horrendous financial crisis for almost every economy in the world. But as the guardians and watchdogs of civil society, it is up to journalists to keep examining the execution of these policies in terms of the following parameters:

- Is the framework still there?
- How successful have these aims been?
- What changes were forced to be made?
- Have government policies given a boost to the SME sector?

If governments' claims are true (and the overall SME statistics seem to bear them out), then there are some good global news stories to be had. If not, then there is a story in explaining to readers and viewers why the corner shop next door to them in any major economy was forced to close last week.

One of the back-breaking but essential tasks of a business journalist is to examine carefully a government's record of fulfillment against its claims and policies. What the government says it is going to do is often clearly laid out but not always implemented. Governments in any country are not noted for admitting to mistakes unless they have to. Generally it is opposition parties in democratic countries who challenge government policy, but the role of journalists is equally important in comparing policy statements against reality.

Examples of SME Policies

Contained in the following sections are official statements of national SME policies by the governments of the United States and the United Kingdom. As you read these sections, be alert to the pertinent journalistic questions: Do the government's stated aims match up to the reality? If not, why not? So why not investigate?

United States

The website of the Office of the US Trade Representative (USTR) states[1]:

> Small businesses are the backbone of the U.S. economy and the primary source of jobs for Americans. Small- and medium-sized enterprises (SMEs) also account for the largest group of U.S. exporters and are a major user of imported goods. In October 2009, USTR launched a new trade policy initiative to enable SMEs to grow their businesses and generate jobs through international trade. An agency-wide working group is ensuring that policymaking and enforcement better serve small- and medium-sized enterprises. USTR has also requested an investigation by the International Trade Commission on the role of small- and medium-sized exporters, to inform trade policy efforts.

This is what the policy is. Such policy statements are easily found on government websites in the early stages of a reporter's research.

---

[1] "Small Business," Office of the United States Trade Representative, http://www.ustr.gov/trade-topics/small-business

In April 2011, eighteen months after the launch of its SME policy initiative, the Office of the USTR, the Commerce Department's International Trade Administration, and the Small Business Administration unveiled the online Free Trade Agreement (FTA) Tariff Tool, officially described as follows[2]:

> Small exporters now have an online resource that streamlines tariff information for 85 percent of goods going to 20 foreign markets with which the U.S. has negotiated trade agreements. This tool makes it easier for small businesses to grow and prosper through exports....

> The U.S. International Trade Commission (ITC) is conducting a series of three USTR-requested investigations to better understand how many of America's small- and medium-sized enterprises export goods and services now, their role in generating employment and economic activity in the U.S., their performance in trade compared to SMEs in other advanced economies, and the particular barriers in foreign markets to the expansion of their trade activity that USTR can address through trade policy. Based on information obtained in these reports and on on-going engagement with small businesses, USTR will seek to set priorities for new trade agreements and for the implementation of existing trade agreements that are more responsive to the needs of these businesses and their workers, so that export promotion programs at other agencies have a better chance to succeed.

> The Office of the U.S. Trade Representative is already assisting U.S. small businesses by removing barriers in the international trading system.

> High tariffs serve as added taxes on U.S. exports and imports, driving up the cost of small businesses' products and narrowing their potential markets.

> The United States is seeking across-the-board tariff reductions and the elimination of tariffs on all industrial and consumer goods through bilateral trade agreements that will benefit all U.S. businesses, large and small.

Any investigation into these claims should make a note of this statement, which suggests that the US government is backing SMEs in a very substantial way. In particular, it says it has eased the burden of import and export tariffs for SMEs. Further, it points to an online resource so that SMEs can check what import taxes have been "streamlined" and that this tool will help SMEs to grow and prosper.

---

[2]Ibid.

THE START OF A STORY

So does the website help? Ask small business associations if it has helped; look at the latest trade figures to see if there are obvious improvements in exports and imports and enquire just what tariffs were reduced and by how much. This at least is the start of a story—so see where it takes you.

The USTR website continues[3]:

> The United States is actively engaged in developing trade agreements that support the growth of e-commerce and the enforceability of electronic transactions....

> USTR is partnering with the Small Business Administration (SBA), the Commerce Department, the Export-Import Bank, and others across the federal government to provide American businesses the resources and the opportunities they need to succeed.

> Working with Congress and other agencies across the government, our objective is to both increase the number of small- and medium-sized businesses that export and to expand the number of markets and customers served by the SMEs that do export.

From a business journalist's perspective, why not put in a call to the Small Business Administration to see how the partnership with the USTR is developing. How and why is it helping SMEs?

The USTR website goes on[4]:

> In order to better understand the key challenges that are constraining U.S. SMEs from fulfilling their export potential, we continue to reach out widely to trade associations and individual companies, from the National Association of Manufacturers, to the National Small Business Association, and to individual SMEs. And we are consulting with economists inside and outside the government, and with our interagency partners, to identify and remove barriers limiting SME exports.

---

[3]Ibid.
[4]Ibid.

As a business journalist, you might want to investigate. What does the National Association of Manufacturers (NAM) and the National Small Business Association (NSBA) think of these initiatives? Get statements from their executives to see if they are happy with what government is doing and ask USTR for some examples, even names of individual companies which the Trade department has "reached out" to.

Finally, the USTR says it is consulting with economists on removing trade barriers. Economists can be the most independent-minded of experts. Track down some of these economists, especially the external ones and see what they have to say.

These claims by government can give rise to a wealth of stories. Without pre-judging what your research might reveal, the chances are that the independent assessments you report will be a lively mix of positive and negative.

United Kingdom

The UK government says that it is doing the following to "make the UK an easier place to do business"[5]:

> We're providing funding and programmes to make loans available to more small businesses, including:
>
> - a scheme with the Bank of England to enable banks and building societies to borrow from them at cheaper rates so that they can then lend to small to medium businesses (SMEs) at lower interest rates
>
> - a new business bank that will provide more funding to SMEs
>
> We're providing funding and programmes to encourage private sector investment in small businesses, including:
>
> - working with private sector investors to provide government and private sector money to invest in SMEs
>
> - investing in SMEs with government and private sector money through the Start-Up Loan Scheme, the Business Finance Partnership and Business Angel Co-Investment Fund

---

[5]"Policy: Making It Easier to Set Up and Grow a Business," Department for Business, Innovation & Skills and HM Treasury, GOV.UK, updated 9 December 2013, https://www.gov.uk/government/policies/making-it-easier-to-set-up-and-grow-a-business--6 and https://www.nationalarchives.gov.uk/doc/open-government-licence/version/2/

We're funding and managing initiatives to encourage young people and give them the skills to set up their own business, including:

- recruiting young business owners to volunteer as enterprise champions who will go into schools and talk to young people about running their own business

- working with schools and colleges to promote schemes such as "Tenner" which gives £10 to each student to start a business and "Enterprise Village" which helps schools to set up businesses

The government has also launched websites that provide information to SMEs on how to run and grow their business.

According to the UK Department for Business, Innovation & Skills and the HM Treasury[6]:

The number of private sector businesses in the UK increased to 4.8 million at the start of 2012—a record high. Barclays estimate there were just under 500,000 business start-ups in England and Wales in 2011; also a record number and 12,700 (2.6%) more than in 2010.

In the same period about 500,000 businesses closed. Businesses have said that they need access to finance and less red tape in order to keep running.

We've developed our policies to support start-ups and SMEs so that they can continue to grow and make a contribution to the economy and so that they get access to finance and support that hasn't been previously available....

Our work covers:

- better regulations to make doing business easier

- working with HM Revenue & Customs to introducing a range of measures to help start-ups and SMEs including a National Insurance holiday for the first year of employing people, reduced Corporation Tax and a Seed Enterprise Investment Scheme (SEIS)

---

[6]Ibid.

- exporting

- skills

- innovation

Skeptical journalists have already challenged some of these claims by the UK government, and stories about banking support through Bank of England lending have been widely criticized.

Were the criticisms justified? Challenge some of these claims by both bankers and governments, talk to sector analysts and economists. Is the UK government living up to the SME support is has publicly stated and has the SME sector benefited from government activities?

Attitudes toward Small Business and Entrepreneurship

The level of small business development in each country depends significantly on that country's attitude toward small business and entrepreneurship in general.

The small business sector develops in each economy under the influence of numerous factors: the macroeconomic situation and the particular demands of the population, the regulatory environment, and so forth. But the capacity of small business to overcome any negative impact of some or all of these factors depends on how governments view the SME sector.

The US, UK, and EU have transparent policies in place to provide support to what they say is an important part of their economic activity. So do SMEs benefit from these seemingly positive policies? The success (or otherwise) of the small business sector depends on each nation's attitude toward entrepreneurial initiatives and the economic environment that encourages entrepreneurial drive.

The journalist's job, of course, is to report on the sector as impartially as possible. Big business often offers epicurean lunches, mahogany-paneled boardroom chats, or chances to test-drive luxury cars. It's human nature that reporters should prefer to examine business while enjoying such creature comforts.

The executives at an SME or a sole trader usually get to the point of the story they want to tell more directly. A sandwich and a bottle of beer is more the order of the day.

It is therefore not unusual that individual companies are ignored and the small business sector perhaps not properly reflected in news bulletins in proportion to its importance. But remember that today's tiny backroom business might be tomorrow's rival to Microsoft.

Even if it isn't, there is a big well of colorful stories ready for the telling—not only entertaining in their own right but more illustrative of the importance of this sector than a mere recital of dry government statistics.

Key Points

- Journalists need to understand the role and importance of SMEs.

- To assess the performance of European national SMEs, compare the statistics for SME performance in the subject country to overall EU data. Analogously in the United States, measure your state against statistics for the US.

- It's important to investigate if domestic governments have lived up to their promulgated policies on SMEs by checking how SMEs perform.

- Examine your country's stated approach in support of SMEs; then ask questions of external entities such as small business associations, analysts, and opposition parties.

- Look for SME stories—they are colorful and occasionally by serendipity prove to be dramatic prologues to the emergence of major businesses.

The Importance of a Census

The economic data that are available to the public in any country can be especially important to business reporters. None are more so than a census. As an example of how this sort of data can and should be used, the census figures in Armenia typify the problems experienced by reporters on smaller and transitional economies. The population numbers of Armenia are a hot topic of debate. Official figures show the country has more than 3 million residents; critics say it is half that.

Why does it matter? Why should economic and business journalists pay attention to the numbers, whatever they are?

The Need for a Census

The fact is that every country needs basic information on its residents for purposes of planning, development, and improvement of quality of life. Statistical information, which serves as the basis for the planning of forecasts, is essential for the democratic process. In the Armenian case, the population figures are a standard by which foreign aid is allocated to the country.

The census is basically a head count of the general population to determine such questions as housing conditions, age, gender, immigration, emigration, marital status, number of children, employment, and so on. The data form a basis of information for purposes of decision making in a variety of areas in the life of residents of the country. All these data come from the official census, usually held once every ten years in most open-market economies but, controversially, less frequently in Armenia.

CENSUS DATA IN THE US AND THE UK

In the United States, the national census is taken by the US Census Bureau. The last time a full population census was run was in 2010, but the Bureau takes surveys for other government agencies such as employment, crime statistics, housing needs, and so forth much more frequently.

The last British census under the old system took place in 2011, and it is the country's Office for National Statistics (ONS) that undertakes the census. Like its American counterpart, it is responsible for providing a whole range of other economic and demographic data at regular intervals.

Collection of census data in both countries goes back for more than 200 years. But in looking at historic records, American journalists need to be a little cautious because a census was also taken at the state level by a number of states for a good many years.

The census serves as a guide for inward investment. A simple example is international consumer chains. Hamburger manufacturers won't invest in a national franchise if they believe that there are not indeed three million hungry mouths waiting to consume their beef in a bun, but only half that number; likewise with soft drink distributors or international brewers.

Domestically, population figures are used to plan roads. Where do they go to and what volume of traffic are they likely to experience? How many school children are there now and likely to be in the future? Such data is required to plan the school building program, the training of teachers, and the areas of most educational need.

Governments need census figures especially for budgeting purposes. There is no sense in planning for schools for a million children if the country only has a quarter of that number, or provisioning for 250,000 pensioners when the true figure is a million.

Census Information and the National Budget

Unfortunately, the national budget is an item that is highly vulnerable to both corruption and incompetence. Therefore, the economic and business reporter needs to be able to read a government budget and understand adequately what money is being spent where and why.

To accurately determine whether expenditure is being allocated in the proper areas and to monitor that activity, reporters need to know statistics from the census. How many people are there in the country and how is the money being spent on them?

Census information also helps answer questions on government revenues. How much tax money can be expected? And if the figures are inaccurate, what are the consequences, not only for the government but for the individual?

In short, understanding population data and looking for frequent updates, especially through a full census, is an important part of a journalist's job in monitoring government activities.

What Census Information Tells Us

Census information is used by all sections of the community, from national and regional government to town planners, community groups, large and small businesses, and more. The figures can determine electoral boundaries and the distribution of government funds to the regions. They can help plan basic services such as housing, social security, transport, education, industry, shops, and hospitals. The information also lets government see how the cities are growing (or shrinking) and what services will be needed in the future.

In the modern world a key requirement of a census is to disclose the distribution of minority and ethnic groups in a country and the financial implications for the budget process. Similarly, immigration and emigration are important issues. If a country is experiencing a huge influx of people from other countries, it needs to know if the immigrants will bring benefits (greater tax revenues) or problems (lack of housing). Emigration in large numbers means that tax revenues will decrease and services will become more expensive to provide.

There is also the question of transfers from overseas relatives. Many European families receive monies from relatives living outside the country, and this income can be important to a nation's economy. But often, as populations age, these transfers dwindle; and unless the data can alert governments to changes of this nature, its expenditure will be far greater than its income.

The Role of Reporters and Census Information

Economic reporters and, for that matter, those who report on government, shouldn't wait for a census to take place to ask questions and monitor activity. It is always necessary to ask about the questions used on the census forms. While population numbers are the biggest statistic required, individual pieces of the information requested can be controversial and in some countries are deemed to attack the privacy of the individual and enlarge the power of the state. It should be the role of media in any country not only to examine government spending based on census figures but also to demand the fullest public debate on what specific data the census collects.

Governments are often joined by industry and commerce in requiring accurate data. Both domestic and overseas investors need to know the best locations for manufacturing plants, warehouses, stores, and other facilities. They need information to assess potential markets and forecast sales, allocate advertising budgets, and staff numbers. This is all important material for business and economic journalists in pursuit of a story.

Census data is essential for some of the most important decisions made by government planners, social services, and business firms. So the media have a pivotal role in ensuring that a full and untainted census is held on a regular basis and that they use that data to monitor government and business performance in both the economic and social sphere.

What's more, the media should examine whether censuses gather appropriate information for the authorities to ensure that their planning reflects the actions and activities that will keep the country on a path to recovery, prosperity, and a successful transition from the old centrally planned economy of the past.

No More Census?

Even as I write this chapter, I yield to the force of my caveat to young journalists: "The golden rule of journalism is that there is no golden rule." In September 2013, the ONS proposed to do away with the comprehensive UK national census conducted every ten years since 1801, to be replaced by a fluid sampling questionnaire.

But as with many government proposals, in a democratic country, opposition parties and many organizations that rely on the census have accused the government of ending the survey, which in Britain takes place every ten years, to try and hide the truth about the number of immigrants entering the country. Immigration has been hotly debated in the UK, with suggestions that the figures are much higher than reported and the government is lax about trying to control it. The government says it wants to find a less expensive method of counting the population, while critics say it could permit politicians to "bury the truth about immigration numbers."

UK officials also want to tap into the huge databases belonging to the private sector and merge the data with publicly held information. They want to use Google data, supermarket files, and energy companies. If such changes are made, many governments throughout the world will be watching closely how successful these changes are. The cost will undoubtedly be cut, an inviting prospect for a number of countries.

STABILITY OF THE US CENSUS

It is unlikely this sort of debate will take place in the United States, because the power and obligation to implement a census are enshrined in the American Constitution. Apart from the administrative and economic justifications for censuses laid out in this chapter, the US Census is the official basis for equitable apportionment of seats and redrawing of electoral districts on the principle of proportional representation.

Using Census Data in Stories

While many stories rely on the most recent census information, data from past records are often used to illustrate a comparison where the facts demand it.

A major issue in the European Union is the free movement of people, which is one of the key principles of the Union. Some member states, notably Britain, are concerned that the level of immigration from new member states is reaching an unsustainable level.

Therefore, reporters use past census population figures to show how many newcomers to the country are from a particular state. Their reports often carry comparisons year on year and decade on decade to show a sharp increase or decrease in the immigration data to support their argument.

Media also use figures—for instance, on numbers of schools and pupils—in demonstrating that education facilities are bulging at the seams or medical patient statistics to indicate whether sufficient doctors are available or being trained.

Without a census, reporting of this nature would prove very difficult.

The US Census Bureau is now making life easier for reporters than in the past, by putting out a series of press information packs including information on such topics as population movements, the aging of people over a period of time, home ownership numbers, urban versus countryside dwellers, and the growth and patterns of multiracial communities. Previously, reporters had to do much more analytic research themselves. All this information provides enterprising journalists and specialist journalists (education, crime, environment) a wealth of material for national and domestic stories.

Civic organizations concerned with the poor, for example, triggered a flurry of stories in the United States by using 2010 census data to suggest that half the American population was below the poverty line. Reporters who followed up on the claim spawned a series of stories that either showed the data was being manipulated or that the food stamp program helped or didn't help and that urban populations were shifting or remaining static. But all these topics required journalists to access data from the 2010 census to back up the facts about the stories that they were writing.

Key Points

- The census is important not only to aid the democratic process but also to aid inward investment.

- Government and business planning is dependent on an accurate census.

- Reporters should ask questions about the content of a census to ensure it is asking for the right sort of information.

- Census data can point journalists in the direction of many stories in such areas as immigration, education, and old people's facilities.

The Good, the Bad, and the Ugly

Journalism is not an exact science, it bears repeating. There are no rules and regulations for journalists as in, for example, the legal or accounting professions. But there are codes of conduct, which honest journalists should try to follow.

Unfortunately, journalism is such a hotchpotch international community involving untold thousands of "scribes" that it isn't uniformly ethical, accurate, or honest. Fortunately, most news writers and broadcasters it has been my pleasure and privilege to work with fall into the honest and ethical category. But I have also come into contact with others who have had few principles or scruples, have given way to bias or personal feelings, or have been reprehensibly careless of the consequences of what they report.

Think carefully before you publish a story, and decide whether you will be filled with professional pride for a job well done or will toss and turn in your sleep, knowing that your story caused irreparable harm either to a group of people or even just a single individual. Business journalism has a greater chance of ruining lives, businesses, or even governments through bad reporting than almost any other form of journalism.

Following are a few samples of good reporting, bad reporting, and the careless (ugly) reporting that has occurred over the past few years.

Covering the 2008 Financial Crisis

This first example involves the reporting surrounding the economic crisis of 2008. When the economic crisis hit the world that autumn, the airwaves and newspaper pages were filled with stories on the economy. Some were good; some were bad. In the following sections, I'll describe how two different media outlets reported on the same story, to the benefit or detriment of readers.

HEADLINES ON THE GLOBAL FINANCIAL CRISIS

"Worst Crisis Since the 90s with No End Yet in Sight" (*The Wall Street Journal*)

"Financial Crisis Brings Economy to Its Knees" (*Washington Business Journal*)

"Markets in Disarray as Lending Locks Up" (*The Washington Post*)

"Three Weeks That Changed the World" (*The Guardian*)

"Citigroup to Axe 50000" (*London Evening Standard*)

"Bank Collapse Sends Shock Waves Around the World" (*The Times*)

"The Worst Market Crisis in 60 years" (*Financial Times*)

A Bleak Future

An example of very poor reporting of the crisis occurred on one English-language television station that was broadcasting news around the world. This TV news station began its news bulletin on the state of the economy by saying that bankers were facing a bleak future. This was one of three headlines; the other two stories were not related to the economy at all.

The station led off the main part of its bulletin with the economic crisis, which was OK. But then it dealt with this major crisis, which was affecting a large part of its population, by reporting from a bar, where it said bankers and brokers were drowning their sorrows because they were about to lose their jobs. The entire story showed bartenders serving large quantities of cocktails named after various merchant banks that were facing bankruptcy while a number of young men, swilling drinks, bemoaned their fate. No commentary, no informed opinions, no detail of the crisis—just a bunch of people getting drunk.

In this story there was no mention of how the crisis would affect the general population, such as in job losses; or the how the crisis would have such devastating effects on the global economy, such as in bank collapses, inflation, and high interest rates. Instead the story was a light-hearted piece that mourned the bankers' loss of wages and the fact that alcohol would make it less painful.

There was no expert interviewed; in fact, all the sound bites were from the drinkers, who may or may not have been bankers. The piece told the viewer nothing about the crisis in general.

When the station cut back to the studio, the presenter introduced a business analyst to give an explanation of the crisis. That would have been fine, except in this case the analyst, who might reasonably have been presumed by viewers to have been an independent analyst, was the television station's business news editor.

■ **Caution** There is nothing wrong in using expert reporters as long as they are correctly identified. In fact, BBC does this to excess. But suggesting that a news editor is a business analyst is deceitful. The reason analysts are used as commentators is to give an *independent* view of an issue and establish credibility. Using a journalist in this way achieved the opposite.

Overall, the reporting was sloppy, lacked credibility, and demonstrated that the news operation either didn't understand the effect the crisis was having on its country or was completely oblivious to and unsympathetic of the effects on the general populace.

It was extremely poor journalism.

Real Reporting

Another station, which was based in the UK, gave a report on the same day and at roughly the same time with a real feel for the importance of the story. Again there were three headlines. In turn, the headlines showed how markets were tumbling, how jobs across the country were under threat, and what the government proposed to do about it.

The anchor presented the program from the floor of a major brokerage, thus establishing what the story was about; and an independent analyst appeared on screen who explained what was happening to stock markets and why the collapse of stock prices was important.

Next, a report was made live from the center of London to explain the possibility of job losses, the effect on pensions, loss of savings, salary cuts, and other issues affecting the ordinary person.

Finally, the program went live to 10 Downing Street, the home of the British Prime Minister, for a press conference with the Prime Minister himself, who was questioned closely by informed journalists.

All this was illustrated with excellent graphics, news pictures, and interviews with experts. It was a job very well done. The story established huge credibility for the broadcaster and engendered trust for its news bulletins over the next weeks and months as the crisis spiralled out of control.

The comparison of how the same story was handled in two different ways is not nationalist jingoism. It is a simple matter of competence and understanding. The one broadcaster cared about the effect on its audience; the other simply bemoaned the fate of a small portion of its citizenry.

An Example of Careless Reporting

The level of national retail sales is an important indicator of how well an economy is doing. So, as the financial crisis started in 2008, many news reports looked at the statistics being published. However, some journalists seemed to be determined to find an alarming headline no matter what the statistics really said.

One news web site had the headline "UK Retail Sales at Record Low," followed by "A Report on UK Retail Sales Has Posted Its Worst Monthly Reading for 25 years."

The report (from an organization representing businesses) actually said that 46% of retailers questioned had reported a fall in sales. So the majority (54%) must have reported rising or static sales. However, none of this tells readers what the level of sales actually was. Retail sales could not possibly be lower than 25 years ago as the headline said. The economy nearly doubled in size over that time period. Indeed, right at the end of the article was a sentence saying official government retail sales statistics showed a rise.

This report was careless and irresponsible journalism.

An Example of Good Reporting

This same web site as described in the previous section also published a good report on investment in the telecommunications industry in the UK. BT, the privatized former state monopoly telephone company, announced plans to make a huge investment (£1.5 billion) in fiber optic cables. No doubt much of the information in the article came from a press release from BT.

But the journalist made the extra effort to describe what this rather technical announcement meant to ordinary households throughout the country. Citizens would get much faster broadband, depending on where they lived, and would be able to run several computer applications at once, such as downloading high-definition movies, gaming, and working on complex graphics projects. The journalist also made sure to write about the commercial rivals to BT, describing what they were doing to improve their services. The article also described the impact of government policies, such as the level of profits the national telecommunications regulator allows and whether this is sufficient return on capital for such large investments. The journalist also made the effort to call BT and ask follow-up questions.

This journalist turned a dry and technical announcement into an interesting look at how technology is changing our lives and how big commercial firms are fighting it out in the marketplace.

Reporting in Emerging Economies

In some emerging economies, competent business reporting is still like a distant star in the sky. Journalists have become intoxicated with the notion of freedom of the press. But the idea that freedom comes with responsibility has yet to sink in.

In one country, a mobile telephone company was making healthy profits. But journalists had been taught under the previously authoritarian regime that profit equaled corruption. Without much effort at getting the facts, en masse the media began trumpeting this idea and made it a headline story that executives at the phone company were corrupt. When challenged, reporter after reporter used the old excuse, which validates nothing: "But everyone knows this to be true."

This disgraceful attempt at writing a story eventually caused the resignation of the mobile telephone company's chief executive and a less competent replacement taking over. A subsequent investigation by an international team of investigators made up of French, American, and British financial experts showed no evidence of corrupt practices, but it was too late. The CEO had resigned and the damage was done. A big international telecoms company had shown interest in taking a stake, which would have provided the company with much needed investment, but it pulled out because of the negative publicity. Jobs were lost, expansion drew to a standstill, and the country's ability to trade internationally was severely curbed. The overall effect was to set back the country's economic revival by a considerable length of time. (And yet for a considerable time afterward, some journalists continued to boast about their part in the downfall of the CEO, as if they had been successful in one of the great investigative stories of all time.)

Bad, even ignorant reporting such as this can impact on an economy, causing misery and grief because ill-trained and badly prepared media simply want a story.

Perhaps there is some excuse for such shoddy journalism in developing nations, but there was none for another scandal, still rumbling on in the UK, discussed next.

MEDIA AND THE GOVERNMENT

In fairness, some governments spend a great deal of money on trying to develop a fair and free press in emerging economies. But my experience is that their efforts are neutered by putting media programs into the hands of civil servants who know nothing about the media, local officials who can't shrug off the notion that the press should be servile to authority, or people who think "ethics" is a dirty word and use funding to line their own pockets.

Britain's Phone-Hacking Scandal

The phone-hacking scandal in the UK, which rocked the headlines in 2011, also had some ramifications in the United States, but the main impact was in the UK. I'll give a brief outline of what happened.

To get the story, reporters at some British newspapers used modern technology to hack into the mobile phones of celebrities, bankers, politicians, and other noteworthy souls. A police investigation, slow in responding to original charges of hacking, discovered that the practice had become widespread. Eventually, UK Prime Minister David Cameron ordered an inquiry headed by a senior judge, Lord Justice Leveson, which revealed that reporters had routinely hacked into the phones of the British Royal Family, the families of murder victims, and relatives of those killed in the London bombings of July 2005.

The public outcry at this unethical practice led to a very old British newspaper, *The News of the World*, being shut down after publishing for 168 years. Several executives of the owner's publishing empire resigned and, for the first time in its history, the British press was threatened with government regulation. The parent company of the *News of the World*, News International (NI; with its headquarters in New York), owned a number of major media organizations, and resignations were handed in from leading editors at NI's stable of companies including Dow Jones. Dow Jones' parent company, News Corp., was investigated by the FBI and the Department of Justice.

Perhaps the worst aspect of this breakdown in journalistic ethics was an apparent lack of remorse from senior executives of these publications, which might still have the knock-on effect of causing limitations to be imposed on freedom of the press in Britain and beyond.

A Bright Future

While the "Leveson Affair" uncovered some bad and ugly practices in media worldwide, the reporting of the huge financial crisis of the "noughties" was largely exemplary and something of which all media, but especially business media, should be proud.

The world was informed about this major economic tragedy through bold reporting, knowledgeable commentary, and easy-to-read articles that were graphic but technically proficient. And so the world began to understand through the media just what had happened and what the consequences were.

It was a feather in the cap of good journalism, wherever it is practiced.

Key Points

- Poor economic reporting can obscure the truth of a situation.

- Competent and full reporting can explain a complex situation to a broad audience.

- Corrupt reporting can cause irreparable harm to communities and individuals.

- Unethical practices in journalism can damage the entire media industry.

The Pros Speak: Journalists from the East and the West

People either love or loath journalists. There is no in-between. Throughout my career I have had to enter hot debate at dinner parties in which one or other of the guests have argued, "It's all the fault of the media!"—citing the rise in the price of food to the fall of a government as the issue the media fueled.

To the dinner fray, I bring my personal experience. I have worked in numerous countries with authoritarian rulers in charge and have been able to cite many examples of how a press that is not free can't stop excesses by governments determined not to be transparent.

In Romania, for example, I witnessed a piece of video on TV showing a cabinet minister taking a brown paper envelope stuffed with cash from a businessman. The government's response to this was to ban the showing of such videos on television. Yes, there must be responsibility among the press, but a press that is muted because people don't like what they say is a sad press indeed.

On another occasion in Serbia, I hosted a seminar for business journalists and waxed lyrical about a free press and an ethical press. One young journalist threw into the debate his experience with his boss. He was told to cover the opening of a factory. His editor said he was to pick up a press release, not ask questions, and return it to the newspaper, which published it just as it was written by the factory owner.

I expressed my dismay, but his punch line was: "The owner also gave me an envelope with cash in it." I was even more appalled until he said, "The trouble is, the money was my wages."

What would you have done? Happily, much of this sort of conduct is being eradicated in emerging economies. However, there are still regular reports from independent monitors such as the UN and the International Federation of Journalists that governments in emerging economies are backsliding on press freedom and transparency. They had guaranteed these freedoms when they wanted to join organizations such as the European Union, but now they have been given membership, they are beginning to forget those guarantees. So reporters, especially business journalists, must watch out for undue influence from government on how they can report or be censored.

The Joys of Being a Journalist

One of the wonders of being a journalist is the wide range of people you meet. These are often generals, prime ministers, film stars, sports celebrities, and company presidents. But perhaps the greatest joys are the firm friendships you strike up with fellow journalists, especially those you shared experiences with while working in hostile or unfamiliar environments.

Nothing is more pleasing to a "hack" than to stand around a bar and relive old times and tell tall tales. After all, that is what a journalist is—a teller of tales, and sometimes of tall tales.

But this is not often just idle chatter. Dedicated journalists are always discussing the state of the industry, changes in it (good and bad), ideas to make it even more effective, and certainly ways to ward off the threats to freedom experienced by many societies in which transparent reporting doesn't sit well with the establishment.

Over the years I have developed an extensive network. And some of the debates that I have become involved with are far ranging and, from an industry point of view, fascinating. What follows is a sample of some thoughts that have come out of these discussions from journalists of long standing—journalists who have lived by the standards of impartiality and transparency that is in the code of ethics but who have very definite opinions on what the state of journalism is today. And it is remarkable how many of the following opinions expressed by my fellow journalists mirror thoughts I express in the preceding chapters.

Alex Kirby on the Importance of Journalism

Alex Kirby: former BBC editor who headed a news bureau in North Africa before returning to London as BBC Radio's environment correspondent. Kirby now heads up an environmental news agency called Climate News Network.

Journalism certainly matters, if only because governments and the rest of those who seek to run our lives don't like it. They don't like journalism's ability to shine a light on what they try to do in the dark. They don't like our refusal automatically to believe everything they say. Remember the advice from the late Hannen Swaffer, a British writer: "The only question a journalist needs to ask himself when interviewing a politician is this: 'Why is this lying bastard telling me this particular lie at this particular moment?'"

Journalists do their job when they hold the powerful to account. They betray their readers/listeners/viewers when they let themselves become useful microphones for politicians, PR companies, campaigners or armies—or for the entertainment industry.

By all means write about footballers or pop singers or whoever you like. Just don't call it *journalism*. Much journalism in countries like the UK is now a branch of showbiz, and it uses some very dodgy tricks: hacking 'phones, monstering individuals, buying stories. Anyone who behaves like this should be driven out of the trade. But even with these appalling blemishes, journalism which holds the feet of the rich and powerful to the flames is so important that no democracy will survive without it.

Traditional journalism is changing fast, not because of the behaviour of journalists but because of technology and economics. Why print a newspaper when people can read it online? Why, if you can read it online, should you pay for it? But unless you do pay for it somehow, not many proprietors will spend money producing a free service. So niche websites produced by citizen journalists are increasingly filling the yawning chasms which have opened up in the last decade.

I'm fine with that—so long as citizen journalists remember that you can always find someone on the Web who will give you a convenient quote, and that working online requires more skepticism, not less. Oh—and that the job is supremely important, but the journalist isn't important at all…like the colleague who arrived at the scene of an incident and announced himself as a journalist. "Never mind," said a sympathetic bystander. "We've all got to earn a living somehow." Quite right too.

Ann Turner on Having an Open Mind

Ann Turner: former seasoned Reuter's journalist who decided to hop off to Southeast Asia. She now practices as a PR Consultant in Timor Leste.

At 23 years of age, I had achieved a position in television news where I thought that I was "senior" to real senior people. We were covering a hijack at a European airport and I turned round to the cameraman, who had racked up 30 years in the business, and told him to be sure that he rolled when the door of the aircraft opened. He tore me off a strip in front of about 100 other journalists. I thought to myself, "I can either burst into tears here, or walk away crying privately." I took the latter option.

I walked in the blazing sun along the airport perimeter fence for a kilometer or so, until I saw a small snack bar in the distance. I entered and ordered food and drink and asked them to put it all into a cardboard box. I set out back to the press pack. I laid it at his feet. Everyone said, "Awwwww"...but I never forgot the lesson he was trying to teach me. I was lucky to be slapped down so early in my "uppity" phase.

Nowadays, new journos don't often have the opportunity to learn from the "grey heads'" in the business. Their pensions are too expensive for them to be retained in positions where they can share their expertise with the less-experienced people so they end up taking "early retirement." I have never forgotten cameraman Roberto Matteoli and the hard lesson he taught me about respect for experience. He'd done more than a couple of hijackings in his time (this was in the 1980s).

We worked together for a few years after that, and one day on a shoot he asked me, "What do you think I should do?" I felt like I had won the lottery. If you are lucky enough to have a crusty old relic in the corner of the newsroom (and few people are nowadays), take the legacy of their experience, respect them, and pass it on to others. Journalism is complicated. It takes more than one head to wrap around the complicated issues now—and then—and if you pool your resources you can create a story that is worth more than the sum of its parts. Old hands such as NBC's Keith Miller, Richard Burr, and others can attest to this. TV news in the '80s was far superior to what passes for TV journalism today. But of course, an old curmudgeon would say that, eh? ;-)

Bob Eggington on Surviving in the News Business

Bob Eggington: former long-serving senior news editor with the BBC. Eggington now works as a digital news consultant.

So you want a job in the news business? What! Are you crazy? It's going down the tubes, isn't it?

No, I don't think it is. It is in trouble, of course. We're all wearily familiar with its economic problems. What used to be a high-cost, high-profit margin business has become a high-cost, no-margin business. Yet it stumbles on. Why is this? Perhaps the airline industry gives us a clue. Its costs are horrendously large. Profits are hideously difficult to come by. Yet people keep starting new airlines and throwing themselves enthusiastically into making a success of this extremely challenging business. Why is this? Perhaps it's because on a very basic level, people want to fly and need to fly. And many of them also want to make their careers in air travel.

Likewise, on a very basic level, people also want to know and need to know what's going on in the world. And many of them also want to make their careers in journalism. I can't imagine the air travel business coming to an end just because there is not enough money in it. And similarly, I can't imagine the news media coming to an end just because the existing business model has collapsed. But it is certainly changing and the practice of journalism must change with it. How can you take advantage of this to improve your chances of getting a job?

There are many ways, but I will pick out the one that, for me, is most important: the need for journalism to be distinctive, if it is to survive. One effect of the information revolution is that news has become commoditized: now that people can look at hundreds of news sources in just a few minutes, they can see that coverage of the big news events is basically the same, everywhere. With all due respect (and I do mean that) to the BBC, CNN, *The New York Times*, Reuters, and all the rest—they're telling us the same facts, in pretty much the same order. Read one version of a story and you don't need to chase around reading the others: the differences will be marginal. General news has become a commodity, like pork bellies or coffee beans. That, I believe, is why so many providers of general news are struggling. There just isn't the demand for a vast number of near identical suppliers.

If a news organisation is to compete and prosper, it has to find something new to say. That means its journalists have to find something new to say. They have to bring new information, new angles, new insights. So, if you're looking for a job and you want to impress a prospective employer, find a good story that nobody else has got. And if you want to keep your new job—and give your employer a chance to stay in business—keep on finding new stories.

The trouble with the beaten track is that it is beaten. Stay off it. Be a journalist who really does break news. That's the only way to a secure future in and for the news business.

Robert "Bob" Elphick on Writing the First Draft of History

Robert "Bob" Elphick: Reuters and BBC Foreign Correspondent in Moscow and Algiers.

Journalism which has occupied me as well as my father and grandfather and kept us clothed and fed has changed considerably since I was first involved in the 1940s. It was once described as "the first draft of History"—which has always seemed a bit pompous to me. They say nostalgia ain't what it used to be, but I wallow in a bit of it myself from time to time. I've been taking myself back more than half a century to the days when I started in journalism with all its faults, filth and noise and temptations.

It struck me that the craft of making newspapers or news bulletins, or just getting news from the source to the consumer, has altered to such an extent that a modern newsroom is unrecognizable to people like me, brought up in the days when typewriters and hot metal slugs of type were the cutting edge of technology.

It's pretty creepy for us veterans when we walk into newsrooms nowadays and our shoes sink into deep pile carpets and there is a distinct hush broken only by the faint hum of a multitude of video screens and a whispered comment or so from the rather well-dressed people who populate them.

Nobody seems to shout or scream these days like they used to. Maybe in the old days they had to do this to be heard over the tremendous noise levels produced by a room full of sweaty people under stress banging away on typewriters with tele-printers every few yards chattering out their streams of tape.

Is newsgathering better done these days? There's certainly a great deal more of it on offer with daily newspapers of more than a hundred pages on most days. Have historians placed too much reliance on what they find in newspapers of long ago (not to mention of those of today)? Is or was journalism ever the first draft of history?

All these thoughts were chasing their way through the mind during the last conference of the International Association for Media and History (IAMHIST) in Leicester when we were discussing among ourselves what the best novels with journalism at the centre are. They had to be novels because there are hundreds, even thousands, of journalistic memoirs. All these are interesting in their own way, but we wanted to get down to the essence of the question. Are there any good reads which expose the methods by which journalists get the stories and also how they get them back to where they can be printed or broadcast?

Three books come to my mind: *Scoop* by Evelyn Waugh, *The Wire God* by Jack Willard (joint pseudonym of Jack Guinn and Willard C. Haselbush), and *The Kansas City Milkman* by Reynolds Packard. These last two were by professional newsmen. Scoop, the best of these, was written by an already successful novelist who had tried his hand at journalism in his earlier days. Each of these books is set in the days just before and after World War 2.

I would say these were the heydays of print journalism of the old school, when new technology meant teleprinters and Hellschreibers and portable typewriters. It was a different world, well before the days of satellite phones and digital composition on fluorescent screens. You got to where the story was by ship or train and you filed by cable if you were lucky.

It was enough to find a cable head, or even by getting friendly travellers to "pigeon" your story or film by plane to London.

What do these books tell us about those times? They tell us it was more than a little venal; hard drinking was the norm; the search for a story, well-sourced or not, was the be-all and end-all of a journalist's existence; but the unending worry about getting your copy from where you were to where it could be published was the main concern.

It worries me a bit as an old journalist when I hear people and especially academics speak of us as writing the first draft of history. Are scribblers in the Press really that important and are they in the business for influence or just to scratch a living?

Indeed, isn't getting a crust for the family table what really moves most of us even in foreign climes? Here are a few choice aphorisms that I have collected over the years and which describe the essence of the reporters' trade:

- *Duty of an Editor: Separates the wheat from the chaff; and then publishes the chaff.*
  — Rupert Pennant-Rea (Editor, Financial Times, 1992)

- *The most difficult thing about living in Eastern Europe is having to predict the past.*
  — Old Soviet saying

- *Comment is free but facts are sacred.*
  — C. P. Scott, *Manchester Guardian* centenary

- *An armed frontier.*
  — Lord Beaverbrook's description of the divide between politics and journalism

- *Kindly remember that all newspapers are vulgar.*
  — Charles Wintour, as quoted by Simon Jenkins

- *What is a Journalist: someone who stays sober right up to lunchtime.*
  — Godfrey Smith, Ibid.

- *Find out what the bastards are up to and tell the world.*
  —Ibid.

- *Journalism is full of lying, cheating, drunken, cocaine-sniffing, unethical people. It's a wonderful profession.*
  —Daily Mirror Editor Piers Morgan, as quoted in *Cam*, page 3, No 39, Easter Term 2003

- *Advice from Editor: Never a boring story; only a boring correspondent*
  —Quote from *Zanzibar Chest* by Aidan Hartley (Harper Collins)

Anna Di Lellio on Getting the Story

Anna Di Lellio: New York-based freelance journalist, correspondent for Italian paper L'Indipendente, and former Temporary Media Commissioner in Kosovo.

In the summer of 1994, the Football World Cup came to the United States. Toni Damascelli was the sports editor of my newspaper back in Milan, *L'Indipendente*, and he was desperate. It was not enough that the event he and his audience had been impatiently waiting for, for the past four years, was taking place in the only country in the world that could care less about it. He did not have funds for the team of reporters he needed to send to the US to cover the Cup—that is, fill out two pages daily for an entire month.

To make things worse, I was the only US correspondent the newspaper had. I covered culture and politics. As for football, I had not followed it since I was a child, when I sat down in front of our black and white TV to watch my father's team, Internazionale, hopefully beat Liverpool. Toni flew to New York and begrudgingly promoted me sports correspondent on the spot. It wasn't easy.

The Italian forward Roberto Baggio was a star for the Japanese media, but I had no idea who he was. Thankfully, his picture was on the cover of some American magazine and at least I knew what he looked like. It was when someone in the Italian press core heard me ask, "Who is Baresi?"—the very famous defender and captain of the team—that I became the object of incredulous curiosity.

"Who are you?" I was asked in turn by about forty male reporters who were such insiders they were updated even on the smallest joint pain of each player.

It did not help that I was one of only two women covering the Cup for the Italian media. The other, a veteran of many football international tournaments, had become one of the boys. I stood out as a woman who was hopelessly ignorant of football. A double whammy.

Despite my inadequacy, the coverage went on without major glitches. I wrote 2,000 words every day. I reported on soft news, such as the mood of the Italian players, or how their host town of Morristown, New Jersey, lived with their daily training, or how the world media treated the Italian team. As far as "hard news" went, Toni trusted me only with a straight coverage of press conferences. After the first couple of weeks, the other journalists grew accustomed to me hanging around, and so did the players. I began to blend in. And that was when my moment came.

For some days, the gossip circulated around a perceived disagreement between the forward Daniele Massaro and the manager Arrigo Sacchi. Massaro, it seemed, was suffering from some injury. In between matches, there are two types of news that interest a football audience: infighting and the health of players I paid attention.

One early morning, when everyone else was drinking coffee and taking a smoke, I spotted Massaro sitting alone by the side of the training field. I approached him with a smile and asked him about how he felt. He began to talk about his injury and mentioned he had been misunderstood by the manager. I pretended I did not understand and asked for more.

Did Massaro know that even the most harmless-looking journalist is always a journalist? Did he care? I don't know and I can't even remember the substance of the story, but I wrote down everything he said. I made the front page and I was no longer looked at with amused condescension by my colleagues.

Danijela Kozina on Problem Reporting in the Balkans

Danijela Kozina: noted Bosnian journalist.

Concerning the fact that in the last two decades Bosnia and Herzegovina received hundreds of billions of euros for the democratisation of media, today's state isn't on the expected level. There is still big influence of political parties on the media, and media reporting is far from independent and objective.

It is especially visible in pre-election and election period. Media are still dependent of the subvention from different state levels. Because of the bad economic situation, I don't expect that situation will improve in years to come—that kind of influence on objectivities of media and daily reporting.

Last election, president of Republika Srpska, smaller entity of BIH, gave subvention to a few of the biggest media houses in RS. After that last bastion of so called independent journalism fell.

Last situation with ID numbers for babies illustrates in which stage is journalism in our country now.

A few months ago, I was in front of Parliament building when protestors (angry citizens, students, parents of the newborn babies) blocked the Parliament because MPs couldn't make a compromise on law which regulates issuing ID numbers for newborn babies.

Because of that, babies who were born during that period couldn't get ID number and therefore couldn't use healthcare.

I am definitely sure that people had been angry with all MPs not only the representatives from Republika Srpska. They are same for them because they don't do for what they had been payed. But when I opened newspapers the following morning, I was surprised with so obvious twisting of the truth. There were no signs of objective perception of situation. Political parties from RS used this case, with the help of the media, for their daily political goals.

All their statements led to conclusion that they are the victim in that situation. Despite the fact that they shared the same destiny with other MPs and some foreign bankers who happened to participate that same day in a conference that was taking place in Parliament building.

I was shocked by that. And that made me wonder where our profession goes these days. Similar situation is in Federation of Bosnia and Herzegovina.

But despite this gloomy situation in media in Bosnia, there are few of them that are a kind of light on the end of tunnel. One of them is Center for Investigative Journalism. They illustrate what the real task of the journalist and media should be—presenting accurate information, searching for the facts and presenting it to the public in an accurate way, without any political influence.

Fair, independent journalism is essential for a democracy to function well. And by reporting what government, businesses and other institutions do, journalists are a kind of filter that gathers all the hidden and incomprehensible information and presents it to the citizens in a logical way so they could use it to decide everything from whom they should vote for to which university to attend to.

I hope, in a years to come, we will have much more media and journalists of this kind.

Anastasia Haydulina on Experiences of a Young Journalist

Anastasia Haydulina: correspondent for Russia Today TV.

I hope it hasn't happened yet. (My best moment in TV.) It's all relative, isn't it? At one point I thought my best story was filming an Iranian refugee family in a Moscow airport bathroom as they've been living in a transit zone for two years. Later that year because of the coverage the story received globally, the family obtained refugee status in Canada and arrived there safely. It just felt that it wasn't just another daily news story that sees air and gets forgotten immediately after.

A few years back I got an opportunity to host a programme "Decade in Review" on Bloomberg TV—so that can be considered a high point in my career; however, it has hardly been as rewarding as some of the stories I covered while in the field.

Sadly, I always took this job too seriously and didn't have THAT much fun. But I guess the most comical situation that still dominates dinner parties has to do with my coverage of a particular little war and having to discuss my script with an editor with a gun on his desk. Just like that: a news editor with a lack of sense of humour and a weapon on his desk telling me my script was unpatriotic and will never get back on air.

The most important part of being a journalist, I think, is to have an open mind. I think I was at my best as a journalist when I arrived at a story without any script or preconception of what was going on, very early in my career. So many of us these days become "experts" in what they cover, writing a story before it actually happens or deciding on the headline while on the way to the scene because of time constraints, demanding editors, or general cynicism. In my opinion it's so important to be affected by a story.

I think the best of us are the crazies, the idealists, those who still maintain a degree of naiveté. It is the only way to then "sell" the story to your audience.

Alexander Sambuk on the Hazards of Starting a Business News Department

Alexander Sambuk: former Editor of Business News for *Russia Today TV* and part of the startup team.

Unfortunately, at the beginning of the new TV service, the RTV main newsroom had huge problems, such as lack of a professional approach to information which often led to an inability to convert raw video footage into professionally packaged broadcasting products.

Against this background, it was the Business Television unit which within a short time was able to set an example of how to successfully cope with very limited resources and produce a satisfying quality of broadcast output. It was there where young newcomers could learn what events are newsworthy and which of them are non-events, or how this or that information can be in the end transformed into a news story, or what professional criteria are applied to a package story.

Among our innovative practices of editorial activities one can point out, for instance, the rule that the camera team should possibly all the time be used outside the premises, filming interviews or events on location, and to make sure only video material should be regularly (almost non-stop) delivered to our production site. This approach to the organization of the production process was to a great extent dictated by the traffic situation in Moscow where at the beginning most of our filming material was coming from. We had no chance to lose time for car transfers of different crews.

Instead of this, after completing for instance an interview, a reporter would go back to the office with his video whereas another person—producer or reporter—would at the same time head off from the office to a new location for another editorial task where the camera-team were already waiting for him. In this case, the time loss was driven to a minimum and at the same time it allowed us to get as much video material as possible in the typical traffic situation in the Russian capital.

So, during the day, thanks to this practice, we usually had a constant supply of the fresh video material and other information of exclusive character which allowed us to regularly update our business news items.

Behar Zogiani—Lest We Forget the Hazards of Journalism

Behar Zogiani: noted Kosovar journalist. Zogiani was sent to a village where atrocities by Serbian policemen were alleged to have occurred during the war of 1996–99.

For a second I thought I am going into the woods and hide. I walked fast on the asphalt road toward that part of it among big trees, being sure that if I reach there I might feel safer. Being afraid of the police I thought better if I run. But all of a sudden came to my mind that running means provoking police to react.

So, I started playing the role of "a brave man," walking normally in the direction where the asphalt would be covered by trees! I was watching to see if the TV crew would come soon. Every minute was ages long to me. I would look at my watch even twice in a minute. I looked back and in front. I was sure no police saw me. I entered in the bushes and hid in the way that no one can see me being there. I stayed there and tried to see if something moved on the road.

After a few minutes I established that when my crew comes they will not be able to see me either. So, I had no other choice than to get out. They were late by 10 minutes. I became nervous and angry at them for putting me in danger. All of a sudden I saw a big number of police coming from Peja to the village of Leshan. I had no alternative but to walk as "a brave man" and behave being innocent or doing my business.

The police found Zogiani and arrested him.

The police said, "Come with me inside the Police Station because we have prepared some special treatment for you." While entering the building, I tried to explain to them how we are journalists and we should be left to do our job. About 20 policemen were standing with their backs to the walls, looking at us while we were walking between them. We all knew what is going to happen. The uniformed officers started beating us with everything they could. After 20 minutes of nonstop beatings my body didn't react, I didn't feel any pain anymore.

Courage is also required to be a journalist. Zogiani is now a freelance business reporter for a number of national and international news outlets.

Sample Balance Sheet

A *balance sheet* shows what assets and liabilities a company has and where the money came from to finance them (Chapter 18). It is simply a statement of what a company owns and owes at the point in time the accounts were prepared. It is an evaluation put into black and white of a company's worth. It lists the net worth of a company—all it owns, known as *assets*—and everything it owes, called *liabilities*.

What follows is an extract from the consolidated accounts of a leading beverage company in millions of euros.

Share Capital	2,406
Retained Profits	3,174
Profit for the year	840
Other	177
Shareholders' Equity	**6,597**
Long-term provisions	3,282
Bonds and long-term debt	5,405
Long-term (noncurrent) liabilities	**8,687**
Operating payables	1,650
Debt repayable	950
Other	547

Current liabilities	**3,147**
Total shareholders' equity and liabilities	**18,431**
Intangible assets	10,341
Fixed assets	1,608
Other	936
Long-term (noncurrent) assets	**12,885**
Stock (inventories)	3,717
Operating receivables	1,146
Cash	421
Other	262
Current assets	**5,546**
Total assets	**18,431**

Observations: What the Numbers Tell Us

A big international group with complex finances, the enterprise portrayed in this balance sheet has grown through acquiring other companies. It has financed these purchases largely through borrowing: *long-term debt*, as listed in the sample balance sheet. The *fixed assets* (1,608 million euro) are small compared to the *intangible assets* (10,341 million euro), which represent the extra cost or premium paid for control when making the acquisitions.

The notes to the accounts (not shown in a balance sheet, but journalists should look at the overall audited accounts) state that these intangible assets represent the acquisition of well-known beverage brands that have a dominant market position.

Total assets (18,431 million euro) are greater than *total liabilities* (8,687 plus 3,147 million euro). *Current assets* (5,546 million euro) exceed *current liabilities* (3,147 million euro) by a comfortable margin. The group is clearly solvent.

The level of *long-term liabilities* is high at 8,687 million euro compared to *shareholders' equity* of 6,597 million euro, and this represents a risk if the group's sales fall sharply. However, the group's business is relatively stable and protected by strong brand identity. Consumers are unlikely to suddenly reduce their consumption of the group's products even in an economic downturn. Another risk is whether the group will be able to replace the long-term loans when they become due for repayment. This is harder to do in an economic downturn.

This example is of a balance sheet. Reference to the company's stability and brand identity comes from the full accounts and or annual report. But even the balance sheet points the way to good business stories.

The company is stable financially and is international. Will it acquire and/or take over more companies? In which countries will it buy? Will its targets resist a takeover, so that the company will have to resort to a "hostile" bid? If not on the acquisition trail, will the company expand its range of beverages, or will it stage a marketing "push" for one or more of its brands?

Colorful stories can be uncovered in site visits. Visiting journalists to one of this group's subsidiaries, located in the old Soviet Union, are told the story that the subsidiary produced the brandy favored by Sir Winston Churchill. Churchill noticed the quality of the brandy was falling and phoned Premier Stalin to ask why. It appeared the chief chemist had upset the Kremlin and been banished to Siberia. On Churchill's complaint, Stalin had the man returned to the distillery, the quality of the brandy was maintained, and everyone was happy again.

Is this a true story? The company executives swear it's fact.

Na zdorovie!

Index

Get the eBook for only $10!

> Now you can take the weightless companion with you anywhere, anytime. Your purchase of this book entitles you to 3 electronic versions for only $10.

This Apress title will prove so indispensible that you'll want to carry it with you everywhere, which is why we are offering the eBook in 3 formats for only $10 if you have already purchased the print book.

Convenient and fully searchable, the PDF version enables you to easily find and copy code—or perform examples by quickly toggling between instructions and   applications. The MOBI format is ideal for your Kindle, while the ePUB can be utilized on a variety of mobile devices.

Go to www.apress.com/promo/tendollars to purchase your companion eBook.

Other Apress Business Titles You Will Find Useful

Exporting
Delaney
978-1-4302-5791-2

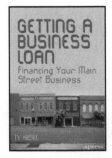

Getting a Business Loan
Kiisel
978-1-4302-4998-6

Have Fun, Get Paid
Duncan
978-1-4302-6100-1

Design Thinking for Entrepreneurs and Small Businesses
Ingle
978-1-4302-6181-0

It's Splitsville
Gross
978-1-4302-5716-5

Healthcare, Insurance, and You
Zamosky
978-1-4302-4953-5

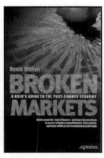

Broken Markets
Mellyn
978-1-4302-4221-5

Reasonably Simple Economics
Osborne
978-1-4302-5941-1

Common Sense
Tanner
978-1-4302-4152-2

Available at www.apress.com

5278803R00138

Printed in Great Britain
by Amazon.co.uk, Ltd.,
Marston Gate.